Old Car Detective

Favourite Stories, 1925 to 1965

Old Car Detective

Favourite Stories, 1925 to 1965

Bill Sherk

DUNDURN
TORONTO

Editor: Shannon Whibbs
Design: Jesse Hooper
Printer: Webcom

Library and Archives Canada Cataloguing in Publication

Sherk, Bill, 1942-
      Old car detective : favourite stories, 1925-1965 / Bill Sherk.

ISBN 978-1-55488-905-1

      1. Automobiles--Humor. 2. Automobiles--Anecdotes. I. Title.

TL146.5.S534 2011   629.22   C2010-907735-0

1   2   3   4   5   15   14   13   12   11

All images have either been donated to the author or come from his personal collection unless otherwise noted.

   Conseil des Arts   Canada Council      ONTARIO ARTS COUNCIL
du Canada   for the Arts   Canada   CONSEIL DES ARTS DE L'ONTARIO

We acknowledge the support of the **Canada Council for the Arts** and the **Ontario Arts Council** for our publishing program. We also acknowledge the financial support of the **Government of Canada** through the **Canada Book Fund** and **Livres Canada Books**, and the **Government of Ontario** through the **Ontario Book Publishers Tax Credit** program, and the **Ontario Media Development Corporation**.

Printed and bound in Canada.
www.dundurn.com

Dundurn Press	Gazelle Book Services Limited	Dundurn Press
3 Church Street, Suite 500	White Cross Mills	2250 Military Road
Toronto, Ontario, Canada	High Town, Lancaster, England	Tonawanda, NY
M5E 1M2	LA1 4XS	U.S.A. 14150

MIX
Paper from
responsible sources
FSC
www.fsc.org   FSC® C004071

To Lady Catherine,
the love of my life.
Her patience and encouragement
made this book a reality.

Contents

Foreword by Bill Gay

When Bill Sherk told me about his latest work, I knew it would be greeted by a whole new generation of vintage automotive enthusiasts. For many, this book could be their first exposure to the man that many, including myself, deem to be Canada's leading authority on old cars and the people who drive them. While Bill Sherk is without doubt a gifted writer and storyteller, he is also a good listener. So when he meets the owners of these cars, he is sure to give them his complete and undivided attention. This skill becomes apparent in this new book because, in fact, he is writing about people as much as their vehicles. Just ask him to tell you about the cars he has owned over the years.

To say that he comes from an automotive background is an understatement. Sherk grew up in the town of Leamington, situated just an hour's drive from Detroit, still the capital of the Big Three automakers: General Motors, Ford, and Chrysler. While still in high school, he landed his first summer job at the local Pontiac-Buick dealership, washing cars on their used car lot. He also pumped gasoline at an Esso station in Toronto while attending university. Having spent a good deal of his working life as a history teacher, he now devotes his full attention to writing about the cars that have shaped the economic and social history of Canada.

I recently saw him driving a 1962 Plymouth convertible through Leamington on a sunny day, test-driving, if you will, the story of the car and its owner for his syndicated newspaper column that now reaches over five hundred thousand readers each week. He has also been a feature writer for *Old Autos* for twenty years and is co-host of *The Auto Stop*, a popular local TV show where his great sense of humour attracts not only car lovers, but also all those people who love the cars that have served as "guideposts" for the special times in their lives.

So enjoy *Old Car Detective: Favourite Stories, 1925 to 1965*, brought to you by the man himself, Bill Sherk.

Bill Gay has been active in the marketing of cars at the retail level. His media career takes in forty-five years in radio, print, and television. He and Bill Sherk have assisted with such automotive events as the Essex Cruise Night and the Heinz Ketchup Cruise. He and Sherk co-host *The Auto Stop*, a popular local TV show about cars and the people who own them.

With Special Thanks

I owe a big debt of thanks to many people who made this book a reality. My editor Shannon Whibbs guided the manuscript through all the steps from my computer disk to the book you are now reading (I was her history teacher in high school!). I also thank Kirk Howard, Beth Bruder, Jesse Hooper, Tammy Mavroudi, and the whole gang at Dundurn Press in Toronto for giving me the opportunity to write another book about old cars and the stories behind them.

Some great stories have no photo to go with them, and in those cases, Ken McGee is the man to see. Located in Goderich, Ontario, McGee operates what is probably Canada's largest collection of automotive literature — and every piece in that collection is for sale. My good friend Ron Pickford told me the hilarious story of an oil-burning 1947 Hudson (see page 123), but took no photos of it when he owned it over fifty years ago. At times like this, I phone Ken McGee at 519-524-5821 and ask Josh or Nicola if they have an original 1947 Hudson sales brochure, from which I could obtain the photo I need. Nine times out of ten, the answer is yes and the item is put in the mail to me the same day.

To the folks at Zippy Print here in my hometown of Leamington, Ontario, how could I ever put this book together without you? To Rob and Sherry Wenzler and to Bradley Collison, many thanks for scanning and emailing photos to our computer — sometimes a dozen or more at a time, and always at 300 dpi. Bradley often has to enhance the photos by removing fold lines or background details, and I'm always amazed at watching him perform his artistry on the screen.

I offer my heartfelt thanks to all the friends and readers who sent me their stories, to all the editors who carry my "Old Car Detective" column in their newspapers, and to all the people behind the scenes, including Bob Cartlidge, Scott Holland, Vern Kipp, Jodi Kish and the gang at *Old Autos*, Alan Paterson, and Mark Ribble. A very special thank you goes to my good friend Bill Gay for writing such an eloquent foreword to this book. I have dedicated my book to Lady Catherine, the love of my life, whose patience and proofreading carried me to the finish line!

Introduction

T his book really got started fifty-two years ago when I bought my first car. I was seventeen and still in high school and couldn't afford a new car so I bought an old car. It was built two years before I was born and had no engine. I had to push it home, but I was very proud of it because it was my first car: a tomato-red 1940 Mercury convertible.

Sometimes, on warm summer nights, I would sit by myself in our family garage (where I was briefly allowed to keep it) and simply sit and stare at it. If only it could talk, I would ask it a million questions: Who was your first owner? What colour were you? Where did you spend your first few years? How many others like you came off the assembly line? Will I be able to fix you up and return you to showroom condition? How long will I have you? I can't imagine I would ever sell you. (I did, but bought it back thirty-nine years later, then sold it again.)

Owning this car and trying to fix it up usually led to disastrous results, both financial and mechanical. But it did put me in touch with other people equally crazy about old cars.

About forty years ago, I met the late Ron Fawcett (1928–2008) in Whitby, Ontario. Ron had rebuilt hundreds of old cars and had hundreds of stories on the tip of his tongue: "The worst car I ever owned," he told me, "was a 1930 Chev. I couldn't start it, steer it, or stop it, and whenever I drove it home, I'd pull into the driveway and climb out while it was still moving and let it roll on ahead till it hit a tree."

Years later, when I mentioned this story to Bob McCracken of Staples, Ontario, he told me that he and some friends piled into an old 1930 Chevrolet and headed up north. They had only gone a few miles when the outside sun visor blew off the car and was too badly damaged to put back on. They looked around for something to replace it with. A sign on a nearby tree said EGGS FOR SALE. It was the same size as the sun visor so they pried it off the tree and stuck it on the car just above the windshield. For the rest of the trip, people kept trying to buy the eggs from them.

As time went by, I began to realize that every old car has a story waiting to be told. And in this age of mass production, when every car on the assembly line looks like every other car, it is refreshing to consider that every car really is unique and unlike any other car in the world because every car goes to a different owner.

For twenty years now, I have been a feature writer for *Old Autos*, a cross-Canada newspaper published twice a month (*www.oldautos.ca*). I write under the byline "Old Car Detective" because my articles focus on the stories behind the cars.

In 2003, Toronto historian Mike Filey asked me to phone Dundurn Press because they wanted to publish a book on old cars and he recommended me for the job. Nine months later, I was thrilled to see my name on the front cover of *60 Years Behind the Wheel: The Cars We Drove in Canada 1900–1960*.

It was published in the fall of 2003 with over two hundred pages of photos and stories of old cars from all across Canada. It soon went into a second printing. On the last page, readers were invited to send in their old car stories for my next book, and many of them did.

In the spring of 2005, Dundurn Press published my next book, *I'll Never Forget My First Car: Stories from Behind the Wheel*.

With two old car books now in print, people across Canada kept sending more old car stories my way, in addition to the ones generated by my column in *Old Autos*.

In 2006, my weekly syndicated "Old Car Detective" column began right here in my hometown of Leamington, Ontario. Within a few months, it was also being published in over thirty other newspapers across Ontario and in Atlantic Canada. More stories rolled in.

In 2010, Dundurn Press asked me to write another book on old cars entitled *Old Car Detective: Favourite Stories, 1925 to 1965*. It has been a pleasure putting this book together, but also a tremendous challenge. I love ALL the stories that people have sent me! How do I pick the stories for this book out of the hundreds now in my collection?

With the book spanning the forty years from 1925 to 1965, I

endeavoured to select at least one story for each year (except for the war years of 1943 to 1945, when no new cars were built). I also wanted to include at least one story from every Canadian province because people all across Canada have stories they wish to share.

The last page in this book invites you to send in your story for the next volume in what could become a cross-Canada series of old car books. I look forward to hearing from you.

Bill Sherk
Leamington, Ontario
September 2010

PART ONE: 1925 to 1942

If you stood on a street corner in any city or town in Canada on a summer's day in 1925 and watched the cars go by, what would you see? Right away, you'd notice the narrow tires, running boards, high road clearance, and vertical windshields. Half the cars would be open cars with buttons for fastening the side curtains. Some cars would have no bumpers and none of the cars would have grilles. The radiator would be in full view at the front, with steam hissing from the rad cap. All spare tires would be in full view, either mounted at the back or along the side. A screeching noise would tell you someone's brakes were worn down. A grinding noise would tell you a novice driver is trying to shift gears (no synchromesh). And if the traffic included a slow poke, you'd hear someone's "ah-OO-gah" horn.

Then came the Great Depression following the stock market crash of 1929. Over the next twelve years, several makes of cars fell by the wayside, including Auburn, Cord, Duesenberg, Durant, Graham, Hupmobile, LaSalle, Marmon, Pierce-Arrow, and Whippet, to name a few.

By 1942, Canada was at war and gas rationing was a part of everyday life. You could stand on that same street corner and see how much cars had changed. You'd see the V-shaped windshields and streamlined car bodies with built-in trunks concealing the spare tire. Fancy grilles with sparkling chrome would help you identify the make and year. Some cars sported radio aerials and you might hear the latest big band songs of the swing era as they rolled by more quietly than the older ones. All new cars now had sealed beam headlights and four-wheel hydraulic brakes. The gearshift lever was now on the steering column for greater comfort when three rode in the front seat. Bodies were wider and covered the running boards, and under the hood was a lot more horsepower. Now turn the page and meet some of the cars that were built during the seventeen years from 1925 to 1942.

CHAPTER ONE

1925 Dodge Wrecker Born Same Year as Owner

Ralph McFarlane of Elmsville, New Brunswick, has long been active in the old car hobby and is a long-standing member of the New Brunswick Antique Car Club. The vehicle he currently owns is a re-creation of a 1925 Dodge wrecker with parts obtained from here and there. Here is the story, penned in his own words in 2009:

> This vehicle and the owner were born the same year, 1925. We both have wrinkles, dents, and battle scars, and both of us know we are not perfect. The reason for making my 1925 Dodge wrecker was to try and make an imitation of an old-time wrecker out of any parts I could find and fit them together into something fairly well-proportioned.

Ralph McFarlane's 1925 Dodge wrecker with assorted parts.

The cab came from a 1925 Dodge four-door sedan. Starting from the front, the bumper comes from a 1928 Plymouth (the first year that Plymouth was manufactured), the front fenders from a 1927 Buick, headlights from a 1928 Dodge, the grille is a piece of crusher screen, the hood louvers were made from the top of an oil space heater, the running boards are made from pieces of grates, and the box is made mostly of pieces of oak, maple, birch, cedar, spruce, and pine. The boom is made from parts of a horse-drawn plough.

There are also smaller parts throughout the vehicle from Ford, Chev, Dodge, etc. The complete drive train is a 1952 Studebaker half-ton except the transmission that came out of a 1946 Studebaker half-ton with a floor shift.

This is the eighth year for this project and I would like to thank my family, friends, and neighbours for everything they have done to get it to this point. I am eighty-four now and it's a toss-up to see whether I finish the project or it finishes me. Lester McKay was down the other day and looked at the truck, then at me and said, "We better get this to the next car show in case you're not around much longer." So thanks to Lester and here we are, as is.

Ralph McFarlane's "Hodge-Podge" Dodge reminds me of my first car, a tomato-red 1940 Mercury convertible which I purchased — minus engine — as a teenager in 1959 in Leamington, Ontario, the Tomato Capital of Canada. I installed a 1957 Chevy V-8 engine from a rolled-over Bel Air sedan, a 1938 Buick Roadmaster floor-shift transmission, and a 1948 Ford rear end. It also had a 1947 Monarch steering wheel, 1948 Chrysler "flip-flop" window cranks, a 1949 Ford push-button radio, and one 1953 Kaiser wheel cover. So many parts made it up that my dad, Frank Sherk, nicknamed my car "57 Varieties," which was rather appropriate because at that time he was president of the H.J. Heinz Company of Canada.

CHAPTER TWO

1926 Model T Ford Found After Putting a Man in Jail

In 1954, Paul Dodington was fifteen years old and living with his parents in Toronto when he got the urge to buy a brass-rad Model T Ford. The brass-rad ones were built from 1908 to around 1915 and were not easy to find by the time Paul wanted one. The family owned a weekend property in Hockley Valley near Orangeville, Ontario, and in January 1954, Paul's mother placed an ad in the *Orangeville Banner* asking anyone if they knew of a brass-rad Model T Ford that young Paul might buy.

Paul Dodington's 1926 Model T Ford is now owned by his nephew, Mike Windsor, of Gravenhurst, Ontario, who restored the car. On a recent outing, Paul is behind the wheel and his brother Ross is in the back seat.

Henry Ford built over 15 million Model T Fords from October 1908 to May 1927, when production finally came to an end because the Model T was getting old and out of date. Les Henry, former curator of the Henry Ford Museum in Dearborn, Michigan, once estimated the Model T survival rate at 2 percent. In other words, 98 percent have disappeared. Two percent may not seem like much until you do the math. Two percent of 15 million is three hundred thousand.

Paul still remembers what happened next:

> A man in Orangeville called us and told us where we
> could find a 1922 T touring. It wasn't a brass-rad T,
> but it was a touring so we decided to follow up on this.
> He kept sending us on wild goose chases out around
> Listowel, but we could never find the alleged car. All
> this was happening in the winter and spring, when
> you couldn't get to the barn where he claimed the
> car to be – snow drifts too high, mud six feet deep....
> He later claimed to know where we could buy a 1911
> brass-rad T. We finally paid him a deposit of $75 for a
> car that didn't exist.

The money was mailed to the man along with a covering letter
from Paul's dad. It gradually became apparent that the Dodingtons
were dealing with a scam artist. There was no brass-rad T, but he had
their money and that was that.

Or was it? Paul's father decided to pursue legal action against the man
and soon discovered this con artist had pulled the same scam on other
people. The Dodingtons took him to court in Orangeville, where the
judge pronounced him guilty as charged and threw him into the slammer.

The Dodingtons left the courthouse and began heading out of
town. Suddenly, Paul spotted a 1926 Model T Ford coach parked on
someone's front lawn with a FOR SALE sign in the window. It was
in running condition for $75. Paul bought it on the spot. That was
Monday, June 28, 1954. The scam artist had unknowingly led Paul to a
Model T after all. He was too young to drive and so the man selling it
offered to drive it to the Dodington property in Hockley Valley, where
it arrived on July 10. It had to be crank-started. The engine backfired
and the crank swung back, breaking Paul's arm and sending him to the
Orangeville hospital. As soon as the doctor looked at his arm, he said,
"That's a Ford fracture. I've seen a lot of those."

Paul's dad drove the car to Toronto from Hockley Valley in October
1954, just after Hurricane Hazel had ripped through the city. When he

reached Thistletown at the northwest corner of Toronto, he passed one stalled car after another on the flooded road. The old T sailed right along because of its high road clearance.

Paul drove the 1926 T to many old car outings, but still kept looking for a brass-rad T. He finally found one in Toronto, a '14 touring, and bought it on Friday, October 4, 1957. That car is now fully restored and Paul still owns it. His nephew, Mike Windsor, acquired the 1926 T many years ago and recently treated it to a full restoration. That car has now been in the same family for fifty-seven years.

CHAPTER THREE

1926 Studebaker Fuel Truck on Manitoba Farm

*B*ob *Jorgenson lives in Stoney Creek, Ontario, and reads my "Old Car Detective" column in the* Hamilton Spectator. *The Jorgensons' 1926 Studebaker was built by the Studebaker Corporation of South Bend, Indiana. Two Studebaker brothers began building covered wagons in that city in 1852 to cash in on the westward tide of settlement that followed the California gold rush of 1849. In 1902, they built their first electric automobiles, switching to gasoline a few years later. Competition from the Big Three in the fifties and early sixties led to the closure of the factory in South Bend in 1964. The last Studebaker automobile was built in Hamilton, Ontario, in 1966. Here's Bob's story about the family Studebaker.*

I was born in 1921 to a large family on a large farm in southern Manitoba. In 1926, Dad bought a new Studebaker four-door with a

1926 Studebaker touring car converted to a fuel truck in the 1930s in Manitoba. Bob Jorgenson is sitting on the fuel drum at the back of the truck. Five of his brothers are also in the picture.

canvas folding top. Five years later, he bought a steel-roofed model and stored the '26 in the machine shed. By the early 1930s, we had two tractors and it was time-consuming bringing the tractors in from the field for refuelling. A fuel truck was badly needed.

The Studebaker was pulled out of the shed and into the work shop, where a complete motor overhaul was done. New tires were put on, the back half of the body was removed, and a rear box installed that held four fuel drums. This made for a very useful utility vehicle, especially during threshing time.

After harvesting, it was time to have some fun! Most of the surrounding towns had a dance hall or barn dance. The Studebaker was ideal for getting to a dance because we never ran out of fuel. Dad dubbed it "the Dancing Truck" and was a little put out when "Jorgenson Bros." was painted on both doors. There was a concern that we were using too much of the gas ordered for the tractors, so it was decided to use the same principle as the John Deere Model D. A small gas tank was installed under the hood for starting and warming up the motor, then we reached under the dash and switched over to the main tank, which had distillate (same as tractors). It was much cheaper than gas.

Antifreeze was a rare commodity in those days, so as it got colder we had to drain the water out of the radiator when not in use. After serving overseas in World War II and on my first visit back to the farm, I noticed the Dancing Truck was missing. My younger brother neglected to drain the rad during freeze-up and the resulting split in the engine block sealed its doom.

The frame and wheels were used to make a rubber tire trailer with a grain box attached. The motor had an interment of sorts. Hydro came to the farm shortly after the war and the motor was buried six feet underground, anchoring a hydro pole guy wire. You might say that after eighty years the motor is still being used.

CHAPTER FOUR

1927 Pontiac Sedan with Back-Seat Urinal

R etired Toronto auto mechanic Gord Hazlett was born in 1919 and loves to tell the story of the urinal he installed in the back seat of his 1929 Buick sedan in the early 1950s.

In those days, drive-in theatres were all the rage in and around Toronto, and Gord and his wife Lorraine often took their four young boys to those movies. No need to pay a babysitter! Gord seldom saw the picture because he would have to take one of the boys to the washroom, then another would have to go a few minutes later, and so on. One night his wife brought a jam jar so the boys could pee into it. The lid got cross-threaded and someone kicked it over during the Bugs Bunny cartoon, spilling the contents all over the back-seat carpet.

After driving his 1927 Pontiac landau sedan for forty years, Gord Hazlett Sr. (right) turned the car over to his son, Gord Jr., who lives in Madoc, Ontario.

Gord finally solved the problem by drilling a two-inch hole into the wooden floorboards of their 1929 Buick, then installed a three-foot length of rad hose with a funnel attached to the top end. Now, whenever one of the boys had to go, he could answer the call of nature while still watching the movie.

One night, the whole family piled into the old Buick and headed for ice cream cones at the Maple Leaf Dairy on Danforth Avenue in the east end of Toronto. It was busy that night and Gord pulled into the line waiting for ice cream. All of a sudden, the driver behind him started blowing his horn. Gord climbed out and went to the car behind him to investigate.

"What's your problem, mister?" Gord asked.

The fellow replied: "I ain't got no problem, but you do. Your gas tank is leaking."

Sure enough, something that looked like gasoline was running all over the pavement and coming from under Gord's car.

He climbed back into his car and told his wife the sad news: "No ice cream for us tonight. Our gas tank is leaking."

His wife began to laugh. "What's so funny?" asked Gord.

"There's nothing wrong with our gas tank," she said. "Little Gordie in the back seat just had a pee."

Gord Hazlett later sold the 1929 Buick sedan for something newer, but kept the rad hose "just in case." In the 1960s, he bought a low-mileage 1927 Pontiac sedan and installed the urinal from the 1929 Buick, then drove to cruise nights and car shows for the next forty years. He has written three hilarious books describing his fifty years in the auto repair trade. You can order his books by calling him at home at 416-421-2014 or by calling *Old Autos* newspaper at 1-800-461-3457. The elder Gord later turned the car over to his son, Gord Hazlett Jr., who lives in Madoc, Ontario. If you're ever up that way and have to use a washroom, I'm sure Gord will be happy to back the car out of the garage for you.

CHAPTER FIVE

1927 Whippet Roof Chopped Off for Queen Elizabeth II

B orn in 1934, Joe Buchanan now lives in Kitchener, Ontario, and is the proud owner of a restored 1928 Model A Ford. He grew up in Sussex, New Brunswick, and got his driver's licence when he was only fourteen, but his driving was restricted to helping his dad with his work installing refrigeration units in ships in Saint John.

In the early 1950s, Joe bought his first car for $15, a blue 1927 Whippet two-door sedan built by the Willys-Overland Company and named after a racing dog.

Queen Elizabeth became our new monarch in February 1952 and her Coronation in June 1953 was celebrated all across Canada.

Joe Buchanan and friends in his "topless" 1927 Whippet in the Sussex, New Brunswick, Coronation Parade in 1953. The Whippet was a low-priced car introduced in 1926 by the Willys-Overland Company to compete with Ford and Chevrolet. The 1929 model featured "finger-tip control" with a horn button that honked the horn when pushed, started the engine when pulled up, and turned on the lights when twisted. It was impractical and prone to failure. With the onset of the Great Depression, car sales plummeted. Willys-Overland survived the ordeal, but the Whippet was discontinued in the early 1930s.

To participate in the local festivities, Joe cut the roof off his Whippet, repainted it red, white, and blue, and entered it in the Coronation Parade in Sussex. It was a big hit in the parade, but with the roof gone, he and his friends had trouble keeping the doors closed. A girl actually fell out once when Joe was driving through Fundy National Park. She tore her skirt, but was otherwise all right.

Going up a hill one day, the old Whippet threw a rod right through the block. It came out by the carburetor and a tongue of flame shot straight up into the air (the hood had been off the car for quite some time). All four occupants including Joe jumped out of the car, which kept rolling along the road by itself.

By the time the four of them caught up to it, the fire had died out. The car itself looked pretty dead, too, so they left it at the side of the road and hitchhiked home. A few days later, Joe received a letter from the Department of Highways instructing him to remove his car from the side of the road.

He arranged for a truck with a flatbed to pick up the car and take it to a scrap dealer. Joe gave the truck driver five dollars for his trouble and the scrap dealer gave Joe five dollars for the car.

CHAPTER SIX

1928 Durant in the Backwoods of British Columbia

*B*ob Hurrell of Granisle, British Columbia, writes:

Hi Bill, I recently purchased your book, *60 Years Behind the Wheel*, and enjoyed it immensely. I once bought a 1928 Durant for the princely sum of $40 from a grouchy old character. After a few days I got around to giving it a going-over and upon removing the back seat, I found a 14K gold "key wound" Hamilton pocket watch and an old crumpled-up $10 bill.

I called the old boy up and was going to tell him that I would return his lost property and his money, but as soon as I said that I was the guy who bought the Durant, he utterly screamed at me: "Don't tell me your #!&*@! troubles! Get lost and don't bother me anymore!" Then he banged the phone down in my ear.

Illustration of 1928 Durant four-door sedan with front-opening "suicide doors" in the rear. Billy Durant formed General Motors in 1908, then was fired by the Board of Directors for over-expansion. He managed to get back in, and then was kicked out again. That's when he began building a car named after himself. Durant Motors did well during the 1920s, but fell victim to the Great Depression by the early 1930s. Bob Hurrell's Durant was probably built in the Canadian branch plant in Leaside (now part of Toronto).

I had a watch maker friend clean up the Hamilton, find a winding key, and a sale to a collector for $85. That plus the ten spot put me $55 to the green side of the ledger and I still had the Durant.

That old Durant made a fine backwoods fishing and hunting car. The long stroke Continental four-cylinder engine would idle over rough terrain in low gear. Borg Warner had a real "granny" low for a three-speed. We drove it to remote lakes and beaver dams, on long unused logging roads, chains on at times in the summer mud, all the places you would take a 4x4 today.

I kept the Durant for a long time, drove it almost as far in low gear as in high, and it hauled out many a fine catch of trout, and deer in the fall. It may have been just an assembled car, but old Billy Durant sold some reliable stuff — Star, Durant, Rugby trucks, etc., and if you kept the revs down, those old Continental fours and sixes lasted forever.

I once bought a '55 Cadillac from a widow. The old boy had expired on the golf course and after the body was removed, his friends threw the deceased gentleman's custom-made golf clubs into the trunk of his Caddy and delivered the car to his wife, who left it sitting in the garage for a year. I bought this low-mileage cream puff, aging but still nice (and fully optioned) for a song.

When I got home, I found the expensive clubs in the trunk. They had cost more than I had paid for the car and I promptly returned them to her. We became lifelong friends and she was a very nice lady.

CHAPTER SEVEN

Learning to Drive on a 1928 Essex

*T*he Essex was a moderately priced car manufactured by the Hudson Motor Car Company from 1919 to 1932. Olge Carss, who now lives in Ottawa, remembers one.

My mother bought a 1928 Essex in 1935. She was a poor widow with three kids living in our grandmother's Toronto home. Mom used the car mainly to try and sell life insurance policies. I would always ride with her on any nighttime calls. I was petrified when a gang of thugs surrounded our car. Only our locked doors kept us safe.

For winter driving, I melted a candle and stuck it to the metal strip above the dashboard. This gave us a wee view ahead. A hot brick in a towel provided very little warmth inside. Years later, we got a small stick-on defroster and a plastic knob for the big wooden steering wheel. All this came from the Canadian Tire store on Yonge Street where the clerks wore roller skates to fetch what you wanted and bring it to the counter.

This 1928 Essex, photographed in Ontario in 1929, will remind Olge Carss of the Essex his mother drove long ago.

"Our old dark green Essex had a metal trunk mounted on a rack at the back. This gave us the chance for an occasional trip. It took twelve hours to drive to Schenectady, New York, to visit old Aunt Jo. We often stopped to relieve ourselves behind clumps of bushes.

By 1940, I was old enough to try my driver's test. Mom took me through Mount Pleasant Cemetery for practice, then took me to Queen's Park for my test. With the examiner in the car with me, I nearly knocked down two nuns as I edged the car from the curb. Failed test #1. Also failed test #2 ("rode the clutch too much"). I somehow managed to pass test #3. Soon after that, I started working for Bell Telephone as an installer. Wonder of wonders! I got a licence to drive one of their little green trucks. Two years later, I was in the RCAF for three years, ending up as a navigator in Bomber Command.

Before starting with Bell, I took my first solo trip in the Essex to go skiing with a girl. It was a dismal experience! I got stuck in the snow and had to get a tow truck to pull us out. I had no money and had to leave the girl as collateral while I took the interurban trolley and streetcar home to get five dollars from my mom to pay for the tow. Then I took the girl home.

CHAPTER EIGHT

1929 Graham-Paige Touring Sixty Years Ago Part One

This photo was taken in 1950 or 1951 when Gord Rieger and two friends, Jack and Allan Graham, owned this very rare 1929 Graham-Paige Model 612 touring car in Hamilton, Ontario. Seated in the car with Gord Rieger are two friends, Jack Graham (who supplied the photo) and Harvey Ritchie. Gord Rieger's son Mark recently purchased a 1929 Graham-Paige Model 827 four-door sedan as a surprise when his dad turned eighty. It was being transported to an auction in Florida when it fell off the trailer it was travelling on. Mark got it at a good price and the car is now stored in his shop in Port Carling, Ontario, where father and son are rebuilding it.

Gord Rieger enjoys reading my "Old Car Detective" column in the *Hamilton Spectator*. He sent me the story of a car he owned over sixty years ago:

> One Saturday afternoon in 1950, two friends of mine (Jack Graham and Alan Graham) pooled their money with me to buy a 1929 Graham-Paige touring car for $225. We bought it from a family on Dundurn Street in Hamilton and the only rust on the car was around the

single tail light at the rear. It was in beautiful condition with a powder-blue body, dark blue fenders, cream spoke wheels and wide whitewall tires.

One Sunday morning, five of us then-teenage boys headed off to Sauble Beach for the day. We were stopped by the O.P.P. near Durham for speeding. The officer asked how fast we were going and I replied we had just bought the car and the speedometer was reading forty-six (the speed limit then was fifty). He then explained that he and the other officer had been doing over sixty to catch up to us.

The one officer was quite impressed with the condition of the car and asked me to start it up. When I told him it was already running, he opened the hood to see for himself. The car was powered by a 6-cylinder "Red Seal" Continental engine. The officers finally let us go and flashed their lights whenever we passed them again.

To modernize the old car, the boys installed sealed beam headlights. They were smaller than the original lenses and so they stuffed newspapers in behind and held them in place with metal rings from a stove pipe. The lights were always out of alignment and the police often stopped them for this. Gord recalls:

I remember one summer day with the five of us leaving Owen Sound and heading for Sauble Beach. In those days, dozens of teenagers hitchhiked. By the time we reached the beach, there were twenty-eight kids in or on the car — the five of us boys and twenty-three girls! The Sauble Beach police in their black 1949 Ford passed us with a wave and a "Take it easy."

Back then, we could drive along the beach on a week-day with two wheels in the water and send up sprays fifteen feet high. After a swim, it was off to the

Beachcomber Restaurant for a cheeseburger, fries, and a chocolate milk shake, then get cleaned up for the dance. Those were the days — no booze, no drugs, and not much money needed. The insurance on the car cost $36 per year. We finally sold it to someone on Weir Avenue in the east end of Hamilton and never saw it again.

Reproduced here is the only known photo taken of Gord Rieger's 1929 Graham-Paige Model 612 touring car when he owned it sixty years ago. With the picture slightly out of focus, I decided to do some detective work to see if I could find someone who owns a restored example of this rare car. The next story in this book describes the amazing result of that search.

CHAPTER NINE

1929 Graham-Paige Touring Found Sixty Years Later Part Two

To go with Gord Rieger's story on the previous page, I wanted to find someone who owned a restored 1929 Graham-Paige Model 612 touring in the hopes of getting a sharp and clear photo of one of these rare cars. I started my search with a phone call to Doug Greer of Greer Restorations near Cobourg, Ontario. Doug has restored many Graham and Graham-Paige automobiles and he told me that someone in Washington State owns a fully restored example of the car I was looking for.

He also told me a 1929 Graham-Paige Model 612 touring was currently being restored at Tom Patterson's shop in nearby Newtonville. The owner was a man from Hamilton whose family had owned the car many years earlier. I phoned Tom Patterson, who told me the owner was Frank Bowland. Before calling Frank, I checked with Gord Rieger. Did his car have a three-speed (Model 612) or four-speed (Model 615) transmission? He remembered it was a three-speed, the same model as the one being restored. Could it be the same car owned by Gord Rieger sixty years ago?

I phoned Frank Bowland in Hamilton. I told him about Gord Rieger buying a 1929 Graham-Paige in 1950 and then selling it to someone on Weir Ave. in the east end of Hamilton a year or so later. Frank told me he and his older brother Joe were teenagers when Joe bought a 1929 Graham-Paige touring in September 1951. The Bowlands at that time were living on Weir Ave. Bingo! Frank's car was the same car that Gord Rieger had owned long ago.

Joe and Frank drove all over in that car after buying it from Gord Rieger. Then Joe began to take it apart to fix it up but only got as far as removing the rad. Around 1961 Walt Teufel bought the car from Joe, restored it in red and black, and displayed it at Expo '67 in Montreal. The last plates on the car were "1971" when it was damaged in a garage fire. It sat in storage for over thirty years until Frank bought it in 2005 and sent it to Tom Patterson in Newtonville for restoration.

That restoration is now complete and the car is beautiful! Its first outing was the July 1st Canada Day parade in Bobcaygeon, Ontario, where Joe Bowland lives today. Gord Rieger is delighted to know that his long-ago Graham-Paige has survived all these years and is now back in showroom condition.

CHAPTER TEN

1929 Graham-Paige Home Again in Hamilton Part Three

Photo courtesy of Image is Everything Photography.com.

Frank and Donna Bowland's beautifully restored 1929 Graham-Paige Model 612 touring car was recently displayed alongside this Second World War B25 bomber (nicknamed "Hot Gen") at the Canadian Warplane Heritage Museum in Mount Hope, Ontario. This is the same car purchased in 1950 in Hamilton by Gord Rieger and friends, who sold it a year later to Frank's older brother, Joe Bowland.

With Frank Bowland's 1929 Graham-Paige touring now back in Hamilton, Ontario, the car is enjoying a new lease on life. As mentioned earlier, its first outing was in the July 1st parade in Bobcaygeon, Ontario, where Joe Bowland (Frank's older brother and previous owner of the car) now lives.

Since then, Frank has taken his 1929 Graham-Paige to several car shows, including the annual Graham-Paige Owners Club show in the Finger Lakes region of New York State, where his car earned a very prestigious second prize for its restoration and won the "People's Choice" award as the most popular car at the show! It might have won first prize, but the work on the other car was done by the owner himself, and that tipped the scales in his favour. Otherwise, the two cars were virtually equal in quality.

At a recent show in Niagara Falls, Ontario, where over five hundred cars were shown, Frank's Graham-Paige won First in Class. This car will undoubtedly continue to win awards at every show it attends. Also very rewarding is the pleasure that Frank and Donna Bowland enjoy in giving rides to family and friends who rode in that very same car over fifty years ago. Frank's sister Lillian, now ninety-two, sat in the back seat and went for a ride. A short lady, she exclaimed: "My feet won't go to the floor!"

Frank Bowland's car is very rare. In working on this story, I contacted the Graham Owner's Club International (GOCI) website at *www.graham-paige.com*. I wanted to know how many of these cars still exist. I was told that the club knows of only four: the previously mentioned restored one in Washington State, one in Australia, one in Germany, and the one owned by Frank Bowland in Ontario.

Frank still has the handwritten bill of sale from the purchase of the car in 1951 and also from when the car was sold ten years later. He also has a document indicating that when new, the car was shipped from Detroit to Toronto. In publishing the amazing story of this car in this book, we hope that someone will come forward with information revealing the identity of the person who bought it new in 1929.

CHAPTER ELEVEN

Old Car Near Antigonish, Nova Scotia: What Kind Is It?

In early 2009, Richard Breen of Antigonish, Nova Scotia, sent me some photos of an old car rusting away in a field near where he lives. The car has been sitting in the open for so long that no one in the area seems to know the make or year or why it was abandoned.

A plate on the firewall reads: PATENTED 1926. Other than that, no nameplate appears anywhere on the car to indicate the make or year or the company that built it. The fabric top has rotted away, along with the wooden ribs that were under it, causing the body to spread apart, and one door has already fallen off. All closed cars in the 1920s had fabric insert roofs because no car companies had yet installed steel presses large enough to stamp out an entire roof.

It's a very big car with a long wheelbase and must have been fairly expensive when new. The radiator and rad shell (where the make of the car usually appeared) are missing and the four-piece hood has been

This old car contains several clues as to its identity, including the rear-hinged "suicide" doors with piano-style hinges.

tossed onto the ground on the driver's side. One large headlight shell still remains on the car, and a metal tire cover rests against the passenger side of the cowl.

All of the seats are missing, but the four-spoke steering wheel is still there, along with a cluster of instruments in the centre of the dashboard. One door panel still has the inner door handle and the handle for winding up the window. On each handle, elaborately carved in metal, is the shape of a pine cone. This design also appears on the instrument cluster on the dashboard.

Richard Breen asked me if I could identify the car. I was not sure what it was and so I asked the readers of my "Old Car Detective" newspaper column to help. You'll find the answer to this mystery on the next page.

CHAPTER TWELVE

Mystery Car Identified as a 1929 Hudson

T he mystery car rusting away in a field near Antigonish, Nova Scotia, and featured in my "Old Car Detective" newspaper column, has been positively identified as a 1929 Hudson Model R Standard sedan. Ted Fox of Brighton, Michigan, owns a restored example of this model, and he supplied the photo you see here to show us what the old car in the field looked like when it was new.

The mystery car prompted several emails and letters. Guesses ranged from a 1926 Wills Sainte Claire to a 1934 Chrysler, with a 1929 Essex coming closest without hitting the bull's eye (the Essex was built by Hudson). The design of the engine was at first a source of confusion, and prompted yours truly to suggest the car might be a McLaughlin-Buick because those cars always had overhead valve engines, and the old car in the field appeared to have one. That guess was only half right. The 1929 Hudson has an F-head engine, which has intake valves in the head and exhaust valves in the block.

This beautifully restored 1929 Hudson Model R Standard sedan is owned by Ted Fox of Brighton, Michigan. It is identical to the old Hudson rusting away in a field in Nova Scotia.

The double row of louvers on the side panels of the hood is another clue to the car's identity. So also is the design of the front and rear bumpers, which are spread slightly apart in the middle. The pine cone design on the instrument panel and the inside door handles and window cranks was used by Hudson in 1929 on its regular production models, of which our feature car is an example. Custom-bodied Hudsons were fancier and used a rose design. The four front-opening "suicide doors" with piano-style hinges are a feature of the 1929 Hudson Model R Standard sedan, and this also is a feature of the car in the field. The fancier Model R Town sedan has front doors hinged at the front.

The Hudson Motor Car Company was formed 102 years ago, with the first production Hudson completed on July 3, 1909. The car was named for Detroit department store magnate J.L. Hudson, who put up most of the money to get the company started. The Hudson was a proud marque for nearly fifty years. It merged with Nash in 1954 to create American Motors. The last Hudson was built at the end of the 1957 model year, a casualty of competition from the Big Three.

On September 23, 2009, the Antigonish *Casket* published a story I wrote about the 1929 Hudson rusting away in a nearby field. At the end of the story, I asked if anyone living around Antigonish, Nova Scotia, remembered who owned this car.

Ralph McIntosh lives near Antigonish and phoned *The Casket* the same day the story appeared. His phone number was passed along to me. I called him and was delighted to learn that he not only knew the identity of the man who owned the car, but also remembers riding in it as a young boy over seventy years ago!

The owner of the 1929 Hudson was a man named Alec Gillis, who lived on a nearby farm and was employed by a company in the United States, possibly a telephone company. He may have bought the Hudson in the States. He never married, but became a close friend of the McIntosh family and often sat in the rocking chair in their living room. He took the children for rides in his car and Ralph can remember how big it was and how smooth the ride was, even over gravel roads. It was green, the same colour as the restored Hudson we located in Michigan. Alec Gillis died in 1953.

CHAPTER THIRTEEN

He Drives His Model A Ford Everywhere!

P aul Wilson's 1930 Model A Ford Tudor came into the Wilson family in 1966 when his father, Harold Wilson, heard about an old car stored in a barn about twenty miles north of Guelph, Ontario. It had apparently been off the road since the 1950s and was pretty rough. Paul's dad bought it and brought it home to Kitchener, where he put it up on concrete blocks in the family's one-car garage to await restoration. Paul was ten years old at the time.

Now fast forward to 1995. In Paul's own words: "The Model A is still untouched in my parents' garage. By this time, I'm married, three kids, my own house, and my parents are retired. After my dad suffered a stroke that limited his movement, he and my mother moved into a smaller house with less maintenance. And guess what! The Model A had to go! He let me have it if I promised to keep it original, which I agreed to do."

En route to the big Old Autos car show in Bothwell, Ontario, in 2009, Paul stopped for gas in Ridgetown. The young man standing behind Paul had never seen a Model A Ford up close before and was astounded to see that the gas goes in just ahead of the windshield.

The total frame-off restoration took six years. Paul joined the Kitchener chapter of the Model A Owners of Canada Inc. (*www.modelaowners.com.*) and the help and advice he received from fellow club members was invaluable. The restoration was completed by 2001. Over the next few years, Paul drove his Model A on many club excursions, and soon logged over five thousand miles. In August 2009, when he and Roxanne drove it on a camping trip to Leamington and Pelee Island, the odometer turned over at ten thousand!

On Saturday, August 9, 2009, Catherine and I met Paul and Roxanne at their campsite near Leamington and headed off to the big annual car show in Bothwell, Ontario, hosted by *Old Autos* newspaper, with lucky me riding passenger with Paul in the Model A, and Roxanne and Catherine following in Catherine's modern car. It was the first time I had had an extended ride in a Model A and I loved it! The car was solid and tight, no rattles or shakes, just the way it must have been when it rolled off the assembly line seventy-nine years earlier.

We stopped for gas in Ridgetown. Then to my utter delight, Paul let me drive his car the rest of the way to Bothwell. What a treat! Many thanks. We arrived in pouring rain and took shelter under the *Old Autos* tent and had a wonderful time.

CHAPTER FOURTEEN

Model A Ford Coupe the "People's Choice" at A&W

Harold Enns lives near Leamington, Ontario, and owns a beautifully restored 1930 Model A Ford coupe. In the summer of 2009, he frequently brought the car to the local A&W cruise nights. I chatted with Harold at one of those cruise nights, when his car was the only one there that was built before the Second World War. Nearly all the other cars were muscle cars from the 1960s and 1970s, prompting Harold to say to me: "My car looks out of place. Maybe I shouldn't bring it here anymore."

That prompted me to reply, "All the more reason to bring your car here every Wednesday night. Your Model A Ford reminds people that Henry Ford built millions of Model As from 1928 to 1931, and thousands of them are still on the road, including yours."

Harold took my words to heart and brought his Model A out to every cruise night for the rest of the summer. In 2010, the A&W cruise

Harold Enns with his 1930 Model A Ford coupe at the A&W takeout window in Leamington, Ontario, after winning the "People's Choice" award.

nights began again around the middle of May and Harold displayed his Model A again. At one of the first cruise nights of the new season, people voted for the car they liked the best. Imagine Harold's surprise when it was announced over the PA system that the "People's Choice" award for that evening would go to Harold Enns and his 1930 Model A Ford coupe!

The smile on Harold's face was a mile wide as the crowd gave him a thunderous round of applause. He then drove up to the take-out window. The girls inside had never served a Model A Ford before and they were thrilled.

CHAPTER FIFTEEN

1930 Model A Ford Roadster in Smith Family Since 1957

On December 7, 2009, I received an email from John Smith of Orillia, Ontario. It read: "Hi, Bill: I read your 'Old Car Detective' column in *Old Autos* newspaper and enjoy it very much. Could you help me do some detective work on my 1930 Model A Ford roadster? It has been in our family over fifty years, ever since my dad (the late Gord Smith) acquired it from a young man in Scarborough, Ontario, in 1957."

In that year of 1957, John was travelling with his parents in their 1937 Rolls-Royce on the first London to Brighton Tour through southern Ontario when his father spotted an original-looking 1930 Model A Ford roadster in the east end of Toronto. A young man owned it and was going to cut it up into a hot rod, but would rather have a Model A coupe for that purpose. By good luck, John's father

John Smith with the 1930 Model A Ford roadster purchased by his father in 1957 and still in the same family to this day.

had recently purchased a nice original Model A Ford coupe in Orillia. He swapped the coupe for the roadster and young John remembers riding home in it.

While attending high school in the 1930s in Galt, Ontario (now part of Cambridge), Gord Smith had owned a 1930 Model A Ford roadster and dated his future wife Jean in that car. When he saw the one in Toronto in 1957, he just had to have it. He fixed it up for Jean, who picked out the colour (a nice shade of yellow) and she drove the car everywhere for years. Their children grew up with the car and John eventually acquired it from his sister.

It has now received another restoration, and documents indicate that it was built in Toronto at the old Ford plant at Danforth and Victoria Park (now the site of a shopping plaza). John has always wondered about the previous history of the car before his dad bought it, and that prompted him to contact me for some detective work. All he knew about the previous owner was his name: Ninian McMaster, Jr. Every attempt on his part to locate that man had turned up nothing.

Armed with the history of the car since 1957, I wrote a big article on John's Model A, which was published in *Old Autos* on Monday, April 5, 2010, under the title: "Who Remembers Ninian McMaster and his Model A Roadster?" Later that same day, Al Sargent phoned me from Cannington, Ontario, to say that Ninian McMaster lives in nearby Coboconk. He gave me his number and I called him. Bingo! He was the man who sold the roadster to John's dad in 1957, and he was now living only forty miles from John.

Needless to say, John phoned Ninian and they were delighted to talk to one another. Ninian had purchased the car from the original owner who was finally too old to keep driving. When Ninian drove off with it, the man and his wife were crying. By the time you read this, John and Ninian will have gotten together for a ride in the 1930 Model A Ford roadster, the car that shows no sign of ever slowing down.

CHAPTER SIXTEEN

Two Weddings with a 1930 Oldsmobile

Rick Herbert of Grimsby, Ontario, enjoys reading my "Old Car Detective" column in the *Hamilton Spectator*. He has contributed several old car stories to the column, including this one:

> My older brother Barry bought a 1930 Oldsmobile four-door sedan in 1953 for $65 from a friend's father who lived on a farm near Crystal Beach, Ontario, where we lived. It had been stored in a barn for several years and was not in the cleanest condition. Barry put some kerosene in the engine and it ran for a few seconds to clean it out. He then cleaned up the car and

Barry Herbert repainted his 1930 Oldsmobile four-door sedan in the 1950s with a brush from Canadian Tire. Under the hood was the old reliable flathead 6-cylinder powerplant with 197 cubic inches cranking out 62 horsepower. The side-mounted spare tire was an extra-cost option.

got some used parts that were needed from an auto salvage yard in a nearby town.

He painted the car light grey with black trim, using a brush and Canadian Tire brushable auto paint. The wheel spokes were made of wood so they were stripped and varnished and the wheel rims were painted red. When finished, it was a great-looking car.

In the winter, when it was stored outside and not driven, we smeared Vaseline on the grille and other chrome parts to protect them. The person who bought the car new in 1930 used it for his wedding, and when we took out the back seat for cleaning, there was still some confetti there. My brother was the third owner of the car.

The most common problem was keeping good tires on the car since they were always going flat. Luckily, there were two spares in the front fenders. Once, when my brother was teaching a girlfriend to drive, she drove straight into a tree and the Olds just bounced back because of the spring steel bumper. On another occasion, a friend slammed the passenger door and the window broke and fell into his lap in one piece since the windows and windshield were only plate glass.

Being a younger brother, I sometimes wanted to go places with my older brother but he did not always want me tagging along. One day when he was going to visit a friend, I crouched down behind the back seat. After driving a few blocks, he spotted me, turned the car around, and promptly delivered me back home.

My brother was married in 1958 and they honeymooned in Niagara Falls with a more modern car. I decorated the Olds with pink and white streamers and a sign saying "Just Married." He took the car for a short drive around our town, so the car was once again used for a wedding of sorts. The 1930 Olds was very reliable, but after my brother moved away, it was not used much anymore and was finally sold around 1960.

In 1897, Ransom Eli Olds began building gasoline-powered Oldsmobiles at his plant in Lansing, Michigan. Four years later, he began turning out his famous Curved Dash Olds at his Detroit factory and it became the first bestselling car in America. In 1904, following a dispute with his financial backers, Mr. Olds left and formed a rival company that built the REO automobile (named after his initials). Thus he had the distinction of two separate car companies manufacturing cars named after him. The REO cars remained in production until the mid-1930s. Oldsmobile joined General Motors in 1908, when that company was first formed. GM no longer builds the Oldsmobile, but that nameplate lasted for over one hundred years.

CHAPTER SEVENTEEN

Bert Powell's 1930 Packard Sedan: Where Is It Today?

*K*eith Powell fondly remembers a car owned by his dad, Bert Powell of Hamilton, Ontario.

My dad's favourite car was his 1930 Packard seven-passenger sedan with fold-up seats, straight-eight engine, four-speed floor shift, suicide doors, no trunk but a rack on the back to carry one, and a microphone in the back seat to talk to the driver (which never worked while we owned the car).

Bert Powell and an attractive young model with his 1930 Packard seven-passenger sedan were photographed by Bochsler Studios of Hamilton for Firestone Tires in 1959. A nosey neighbour couldn't resist taking a picture of his own. The battery was in a box in the right front fender for ease of checking. If you had sidemount tires as shown here, you had to remove the tire before checking the battery.

Our family used to go for rides in this car when I was a young boy, and we travelled to many small towns in southern Ontario. We belonged to a club called the HCCA or Horseless Carriage Club of America (current Canadian website address: *http://hcca.org/regions. php#CANADA*).

My dad bought the Packard in early 1957 for $125. He found it in a farmer's field and had it towed to his garage at work and restored it as best he could to the condition in the picture. We had a place to park it behind our home on Miles Court in Hamilton.

The car was sold around 1970 to another club member, I believe, and we simply lost track of it. Unfortunately, the garage behind our home had been taken over by new owners of the property and the old garage was demolished so we had no place to park the car. My dad never really had much money, but it was very difficult for him to give it up. Selling it for a few dollars was the only option since those types of vehicles were not as rare then as they are now. I think he got $600 for it.

I sure miss that car and the times we had going from place to place and meeting other families with old cars. I remember on one trip we got a police escort after dark for several vehicles to come home as the lights on some of the cars either did not work or were not bright enough. The police car broke down so Dad's Packard with its big headlights led the way and everyone got home safe.

Keep up the good work, Bill, if only for the love of those great cars.

James Ward Packard reportedly purchased a new Winton from Alexander Winton in Cleveland, Ohio, around 1898. That Winton, so the story goes, broke down several times while Mr. Packard was attempting to drive it home. He returned it to the factory and told Mr. Winton what he thought of the car. Mr. Winton apparently replied with: "If you're so smart, Mr. Packard, why don't you build a car of your own?"

Mr. Packard did exactly that. The first Packard was completed in November 1899 and the last one was built in 1958. For several decades, Packard was considered by many to be the ultimate American luxury car. Their sales slogan was famous: "Ask the man who owns one."

CHAPTER EIGHTEEN

1931 Chevrolet Coupe Nicknamed the "Green Hornet"

*F*red Marks lives in Brantford, Ontario. Here is his story.

The Green Hornet was a little 1931 Chevrolet two-passenger coupe that I bought in 1952 when entering my second year at the University of Western Ontario in London. It faithfully took me back and forth between home and London for the next three years, and a good many other places in between.

A group of us were playing cards one afternoon and lost track of the time. One of the fellows was heading home for the weekend and had to catch the train to Leamington, and we had only a few minutes to get him to the station. Among us was a fellow named Plato Konduras. Plato could imitate the sound of a siren as shrill and authentic as the latest model. We headed down Richmond Street from the university to the train station at 5:00 p.m. on a Friday afternoon with two friends standing on the running boards and plenty of traffic blocking our way.

Plato took care of that. Every time we pulled up behind a car, he would cut loose with his siren and the car would pull over and let us go

1931 Chevrolet coupe in the sales brochure.

by. When we came to stoplights, the two chaps on the running boards would hop off, run through the intersection, and remount on the other side of the street. It was a real power trip to the station and we made it with a couple of minutes to spare.

When I finished school, the Green Hornet was stored in a coal bin at my father's place of business. Vandals trashed it and it was sent to a scrapyard. An author once wrote: "May your first love be your last love." I knew what he meant because I have never felt the same attachment to any other car that I had for my first one.

CHAPTER NINETEEN

The Astonishing Tale of a 1931 Model A Ford

*A*llan Gravelle of Nepean, Ontario, tells his story.

My first job in 1949 paid only fifty cents an hour. After six months, I had saved enough money to buy my first car, a 1931 Model A Ford. My brother Bob was still in high school and suggested our pal Jack and I should attend Bob's school dance. Because we lived in the country about eight miles from the school, I agreed to drive us to the dance.

The school dance in the gym was well-attended and we knew many of the girls. About ten o'clock Jack asked to use my Model A to drive his girl home. As the dance would not end for another hour, I let him borrow it. The girl lived only a few blocks away and Jack said he would be back soon. When the dance ended, Jack had still not returned. He finally returned just before midnight with an astonishing story.

On the way to his girl's home, the car caught fire under the hood and Jack used my new car-seat blanket to put the fire out. The blanket was ruined, but the car still ran. He drove the girl home, but had

Illustrated Model A Ford sedan.

a fender-bender with her dad's car, which was parked in the drive-way. Jack told her father about the accident and gave him my insur-ance number to pay for the damages. When he returned to the Model A, he found that he had locked the car with the keys in the ignition! Undaunted, he smashed the driver's side window to get the keys.

We had a cool drive home that night. As far as I know, my insur-ance paid for the damage to the other car. Henry Ford made the Model A out of real steel so there was no damage to my car. It cost me only six dollars to replace the window. This story would have ended badly (and with a big bang) if the fire had spread to the gas tank, which is located in the cowl just behind and above the engine in a Model A.

CHAPTER TWENTY

1932 Ford Coupe with One Owner Since 1954

Sam Higginbottom's 1932 Ford five-window coupe rides like a dream and is a dream come true. He was a student at Kennedy Collegiate in Windsor, Ontario, in 1954 when he saw the car for sale on a used car lot for $125. He had saved exactly that amount as a carry-out boy at a local supermarket. Recalls Sam:

> My dad was dead set against it. "Those cars are nothing but trouble," I remember him saying to me. He wanted me to buy a Kaiser-Frazer off the lot because it had a Continental engine, so I really had to persuade my dad that the '32 Ford coupe was the car I wanted.

Sam and Heather Higginbottom pose proudly with their 1932 Ford five-window coupe. Note the Year of Manufacture (YOM) 1932 licence plate, now legal in Ontario. Sam's two brothers also own 1932 Fords. Gary has a hot-rodded roadster and Ken has a two-door sedan. All three are on the road.

Dad came along as part of the deal because I did not yet have my driver's licence and my dad drove the '32 Ford home for him.

It wasn't too long after that when I got my driver's licence. I kept the car original for a while (it was the 4-cylinder Model B), but had the itch to have a real hot rod. I got a '56 Olds engine from a junkyard for $100. It must have had two hundred thousand miles on it because as soon as I put it in and got it running, the engine blew up. I paid $50 for a flathead Ford V-8 and put that in. I then replaced all four fenders with motorcycle fenders.

But the fenders were too close to the tires (they were rubbing) and the original '32 Ford steering was shaking and wobbling so I was really afraid to drive the car much.

Sam parked the car for the next thirty years. He and Heather were married in 1966 and raised two boys. On holidays, they camped all over Canada and the United States. In 1994, Sam retired as an electrician from the Chrysler Corporation with thirty-three years of service. Two years later, his brothers Gary and Ken persuaded him to finally finish the 1932 Ford he had bought so long ago.

Sam's '32 was given a boxed frame, new floor and firewall, a Maverick rear end, front-disc brakes, and a small block Chevy V-8 engine. Reproduction fenders identical to the originals were installed, along with a stainless-steel gas tank and blue dot tail lights. The car was finished inside and out by 2004. Sam and Heather have now driven the car to many shows and cruise nights around Ontario, and it always attracts admiring attention. It's come a long way from that day in 1954 when he saw it for sale on a used-car lot.

For $610 (Windsor factory list), a new Ford Sport Coupe with rumble seat in 1932 gave you a 4-cylinder engine with 50 horsepower. For an extra $60, you could have the first V-8 engine in the low price field with 65 horsepower.

CHAPTER TWENTY-ONE

1933 Chrysler Sedan Rescued from a Cornfield

*C*lem Pudjunas of Hamilton, Ontario, sent in this story.

Hi, Bill. I enjoy your column in the *Hamilton Spectator*. Here is the story behind our 1933 Chrysler Six Model CO sedan.

In the early 1960s, my father purchased this car from a farmer near North Bay, Ontario. The previous owner explained that he found the Chrysler abandoned in the mid-1930s on a road adjacent to his farm. The keys were in the ignition and the car was in good running order. When the farmer reported the abandoned car, the local police asked him to hitch up a team of horses and tow the car to his farm. A year or so passed with no one claiming it, and the farmer was awarded the title

Clem's beautifully restored 1933 Chrysler Six Model CO sedan has many noteworthy features to tempt a new car buyer in 1933, including an all-steel body with Duplate safety glass in the windshield, streamlined front end, adjustable driver's seat, double windshield with two wipers, two adjustable sun visors, and ivory control knobs. You could have all this and more for the Windsor factory list price of $1,180.

to the four-year-old vehicle. He drove it for many years before retiring it to a cornfield.

After my father parted with $65, the car was towed to southern Ontario. The engine and brakes were limbered up and we used the old Chrysler occasionally for short drives to visit relatives or trips to the Dairy Queen. One summer my father packed it full of family and gear and headed up Hwy. 400 to our cottage. The road into the cottage was not the greatest, and Dad much preferred the 1933 Chrysler with its high road clearance. The cottage road was terribly hard on the under-side of our regular car, a 1959 Cadillac.

The 224-cubic-inch long stroke engine provides plenty of low-end torque. Sometimes the old Chrysler was used to haul the hay wagon around on our farm when the tractors were busy raking and baling hay. We would tie the steering wheel to the door post, put it in low gear, and pull the throttle out slightly — and the old car would idle along straight up the field by itself with the wagon in tow while we walked alongside and tossed on bales of hay. Eventually the old car ended up tucked into a corner of the barn for years and we used it to store stacks of chicken feed.

In celebration of Chrysler's 50th year, I began a complete res-toration. This Canadian-built car uses its original 86 hp 6-cylinder flathead engine, drive train, and 6-volt electrical system. The vehicle when new came equipped with hydraulic brakes, dual side mounts, split windshield, full instrumentation, free-wheeling transmission, and 5.50 x 17 wire-spoke wheels.

This seventy-eight-year-old Chrysler still drives smooth after ninety-five thousand miles. We don't use it to pull the hay wagon anymore.

CHAPTER TWENTY-TWO

1933 Dodge in Same Family Since New

Art Fishenden lives in Packenham, Ontario, and enjoys reading my "Old Car Detective" column in his local *EMC* newspaper:

> I would like to share with you the story behind my car. It is an all-original 1933 Dodge Brothers Model DP Deluxe sedan with side mounts, suicide doors, a fold-out windshield, and other extras. It was purchased by my grandfather, John Hiram Barr, in 1933 from S.E. Lewis in Arnprior, Ontario. My grandfather had a very heavy foot, but managed to avoid any serious fender-benders. He used it for transportation and for hauling grain and feed from the mill, and it had a carrier or luggage rack on the back.

Art Fishenden's 1933 Dodge Brothers Model DP Deluxe sedan.

He drove it until about ninety years of age at which time he retired into the village of Packenham. That was around 1958. He gave the car to his youngest daughter, who gave it to me, her nephew. It has never left the family. I drove it for two years, then parked it in an open shed about 1960.

There it sat for forty years until 2000, when my nephew Larry and I decided to restore it. The car was still complete, but in pretty rough shape and with a seized engine. We had no idea of the job that lay ahead. It is really difficult to get replacement parts for Dodge Brothers cars of that era.

It was a frame-off restoration involving body work, major engine rebuilding, new chrome, new glass, new upholstery, many adjustments, and lots of work and money. It was running again for the first time in 2006, then blew the starter motor. Following more adjustments, it was back on the road in 2007. I took it to a couple of car shows and it received two awards, one being Best of Show.

She, my car, now has a new lease on life and has come from a sad heap of rust sinking into the mud to a very beautiful lady of which I am very proud.

Four body styles were available in this series for 1933: the featured car, a five-passenger sedan for $950, a four-passenger coupe with rumble seat for $920, a five-passenger "brougham salon" for $950, and a four-passenger convertible coupe with rumble seat for $980. All prices are "Windsor factory list." By comparison, a 1933 Ford four-door sedan with a V-8 engine had a "Windsor factory list" price of $745.

John and Horace Dodge began building cars bearing their name in November 1914, after supplying parts to other manufacturers, including Ford, for several years. Both brothers became millionaires and both died in 1920. Walter Chrysler bought the Dodge Company in 1928.

Art Fishenden's 1933 Dodge Model DP Deluxe sedan rides on a wheelbase of 115 inches and is powered by a 6-cylinder inline L-head engine mounted on rubber and cranking out 75 horsepower at 3600 rpm from 201.3 cubic inches.

Features include hydraulic four-wheel brakes, a fully insulated all-steel body, safety glass in the windshield, twin trumpet-style horns, and two tail lamps. The instrument panel includes a glove compartment and all control knobs are finished in antique ivory. And all this for a Windsor factory list price of $950!

CHAPTER TWENTY-THREE

1934 Chevrolet Cabriolet from Montreal to Nova Scotia

In 1956 at age twenty-one, John "Jerry" Bartlett bought a 1934 Chevrolet cabriolet in running condition in Montreal for $40. The previous owner had tried selling it to a wrecking yard, but was only offered $15.

"Jerry" Bartlett behind the wheel of his 1934 Chev cabriolet soon after buying it in Montreal for $40 in 1956.

Burt and Lu Fulmore of Economy, Nova Scotia, in their 1934 Chevrolet convertible after buying it from Mr. Bartlett and restoring it. Today it's worth far more than $40!

Jerry later joined the Royal Canadian Navy and was stationed in Halifax. He left the 1934 Chev in Montreal and only drove it when on leave. In 1959, the engine threw a rod, and by this time Jerry had met and married a woman down east. He left the engine behind and towed the Chev to Nova Scotia behind his 1938 McLaughlin-Buick.

For the next thirteen years, he stored the old convertible in one place after another, and at each place, parts disappeared from it. Finally, in 1972, he decided it was too far gone for him to restore and he put it up for sale. It was missing the engine, radiator, grille, seats, top, instruments, and hubcaps, and an old washtub full of parts sat in the car.

Burt Fulmore of Economy, Nova Scotia, bought what was left of the car. For the next three years, he rounded up the missing parts from all across Canada and the United States. Then work on the car began in earnest and the restoration was completed in 1979, seven years after the car was purchased. Over the next twenty-five years, Burt and his wife Lu have taken the car to shows in Canada and the United States and it has won many awards for the quality of the restoration.

Burt knew the car was rare when he bought it. GM of Canada confirmed that only 148 of these convertibles were built in Canada. Burt's car has the optional side-mounted spare tires in the front fenders, a luggage rack on the back, and very rare fender skirts.

The serial number of Burt's car is 642518. Since starting this story, and with Burt's help, I have located two other identical Canadian-built cars. Don and George Elliott of Elliott Auto Parts in Newtonville, Ontario, own a very nice example, which they purchased in June of 1975. Its serial number is 636222, indicating it was built before Burt's car.

Bern Macdonald of Penetanguishene, Ontario, bought one in 1951 for $450, and still owns it! He restored it a few years ago and enjoys driving it. Its serial number is 645601, indicating it was built after Burt's car.

As far as we know, these are the only three surviving examples of the 148 Chevrolet cabriolets built in Canada in 1934. We welcome any leads on others that might still be around.

CHAPTER TWENTY-FOUR

1934 Chevrolet Coach Home After Twenty-Five Years

Gary Greenland and Garry Jr. of Stoney Creek, Ontario, are currently bringing back to life a car that was in their family over twenty-five years ago. It's a wonderful father-and-son story.

Gary (the father) purchased an all-original 1934 Chev Standard coach in 1976 after answering an ad in the *Hamilton Spectator*. At first, he bought it with the intention of turning it into a street rod, but soon decided its excellent original condition should be preserved. For the next five years, Gary and his wife drove it to car shows and swap meets all around southern Ontario with their two young sons, Garry Jr. and Jason.

The Greenlands' 1934 Chevrolet Standard coach is well on the way to being restored and back on the road. Garry (the son) contacted the "Old Car Detective" following an article on Burt Fulmore's restored 1934 Chevrolet cabriolet in Nova Scotia. Garry and Burt got together over the phone and Burt has been giving invaluable advice in aiding the restoration of the Greenlands' 1934 Chevrolet.

The car was reluctantly sold in 1981 owing to hard times (remember when interest rates on mortgages topped twenty percent?). Garry Jr. loved that car and was heartbroken to see it go. At age fifteen, his dad bought him a 1969 Chevelle hardtop, which he still owns. But young Garry never stopped thinking about their long-lost 1934 Chev.

Then one day in 2006, he found a note in the family album that led to a phone call to a man in Selkirk, Ontario. Rick James had purchased the Greenlands' 1934 Chevrolet from another person a few years earlier and had been restoring it. When Garry Jr. called to inquire about it, Rick's wife answered and said her husband was now driving a transport truck and no longer had time to finish the restoration.

Garry drove down to Selkirk and saw the car he had not seen in twenty-five years. A deal was struck and he brought it home. But he didn't tell Mom and Dad. Not yet. He rolled the car into his garage along with all the extra parts that came with it, then went next door (where his parents lived) and mentioned there was something in his garage that they should see.

His mother was the first to look at it. When she realized what it was, she began to cry. When his dad returned home a little later, he also looked at it. At first, he thought it was just an old '34 Chev. Then Jason said: "No, Dad. It's our '34 Chev and it has come back home."

For the next half hour, Dad was speechless as he slowly walked around it and touched it, hardly believing that it was really there. Then he finally spoke: "It's not finished. It still needs work." Father and son are now finishing the restoration of the car that had been gone from their family for a quarter of a century.

CHAPTER TWENTY-FIVE

Alberta Bound in a 1934 Ford V-8

*I*n 1932, Henry Ford introduced the first V-8 engine in the low-priced field. For the next twenty-two years, Ford was unique among the Big Three in offering this engine in that price range. Not until 1955 did Chevrolet and Plymouth catch up to Ford under the hood.

Stan Bendle lives near Kingston, Ontario, and reads my column in the local EMC paper. He still remembers the V-8 engine in his 1934 Ford.

On September 9, 1946, I joined the Royal Canadian Air Force (RCAF), stationed first at Trenton, then at Downsview near Toronto. That's when I bought a 1934 Ford V-8 for $300.

Three weeks later, I threw a connecting rod and put a hole in the cylinder wall. Someone told me that if I could get a block of hardwood to put into the cylinder and plug the hole, the motor might be okay.

I got a piece of wood, removed the head from the motor, hammered the block of wood into the cylinder, and put the head back on. I drove

Stan Bendle with his 1934 Ford V-8 in 1948. When new, his car would have cost $780 as a Standard sedan and $820 as a Deluxe sedan (Windsor factory list prices). Stan Bendle complained about his brakes, which were four-wheel mechanical. Henry Ford stubbornly refused to consider hydraulic brakes well after the other manufacturers had made the switch. As late as 1938, he was boasting of building cars with brakes that gave you "the safety of steel from pedal to wheel." Finally in 1939, Ford made the switch to four-wheel hydraulic brakes.

about a mile and the motor shook and vibrated so much, I bought a reconditioned motor and my '34 Ford V-8 ran well again.

In August 1948, I was informed I would be transferred to Calgary. This meant I could not be best man at my brother's wedding. I put an ad in the *Toronto Daily Star* for paying passengers and two guys came with me to Calgary. I charged them $20 apiece.

My brakes were not very good so I had to start braking well before all the stop signs and traffic lights. Going through the Badlands of North Dakota, I started to hear an awful howl coming from the transmission. We travelled about twenty-five miles at reduced speed before we found a service station where the transmission was filled with oil and the howling stopped. We reached Calgary without further trouble.

Three months later, I was transferred to Edmonton. I remember driving there from Calgary. The motor stopped about every twenty miles so I waited about twenty minutes and it would start again. I finally reached Edmonton and found a repair garage. They said my car needed a new coil and they put one in.

About two weeks later, the senior warrant officer asked me if I had any insurance on my '34 Ford, parked just outside my barrack block. I had to tell him I had no insurance. He said to get insurance or remove my car from DND property. I sure couldn't afford insurance and I had to sell my '34 Ford V-8.

CHAPTER TWENTY-SIX

1935 Ford Coupe Found Twenty-Five Years Later

Many residents of Stratford, Ontario, know Vince Gratton from the years he operated Gratton Auto Body in this city. Older residents still remember Vince's father, Don Gratton, who came to the area from northern Ontario in 1935 and took over a service station in nearby Shakespeare. That business expanded into Gratton Auto Parts and Wrecking Yard, and young Vince grew up surrounded by cars both old and new. When he turned fourteen, his dad decided his son was old enough to have a car of his own. Vince recalls:

Vince Gratton (left) and friend examine the engine in Vince's 1935 Ford three-window coupe in 1959.

Vince Gratton sold his 1935 Ford coupe in 1960 and found it twenty-five years later when owned and refinished all over again by Bob Booth of Fitzroy Harbour in eastern Ontario.

We went over to Saunders Auto Wrecking in Thorndale. The fellow running it back then never junked anything, and all his good cars were lined up at the front. The one I picked was a '35 Ford three-window coupe. The body was absolutely rust-free with original grey paint, typical dents in the fenders, and tarnished chrome. I tried to get the engine running, but the car had a cracked block.

Sometimes I'm amazed when I look back and think, *Where did I find the nerve to tackle such a project?* Over the next two years, I took the whole front end off, then put a '40 Mercury motor in it with dual exhausts, put the battery up on the firewall, rewired the whole car, installed sealed beam headlights with a dimmer switch on the floor, bobbed the fenders, installed '48 Pontiac tail lights on the inner deck, inboard from the fenders, then filled in the seam between the rear fenders and the body. Then I repainted the whole car in a dazzling new 1959 Ford colour — Mauve Metallic.

Over the next few years, Vince bought and sold a steady stream of exciting cars including another 1935 Ford three-window coupe with a Cadillac engine. Fast-forwarding to 1985, Vince says:

> I was at the Barrie Flea Market and a fellow was selling '35 and '36 Ford parts. Given that my '35 was my first car and I still had a real love for it, I got talking to him about how I'd had one, with a '49 Mercury dash with the round gauges all molded in, and the '48 Pontiac taillights. And he said: 'I've got your car!' This was 1985 and I had not seen the car since 1960!
>
> The new owner is well known in the old car hobby. Bob Booth from Fitzroy Harbour near Ottawa has owned dozens of '35–'36 Fords over the years and he restored mine over the past ten or twenty years. It's not for sale, but it's a thrill for me to know that my first car is still out there.

CHAPTER TWENTY-SEVEN

Date Disaster with a 1936 Chevrolet

*D*on Fraser of Ottawa, Ontario, reads my column in the local *Kanata* EMC *paper and sent in his story.*

When the Arts Formal at Queen's University rolled around in January 1945, I was only eighteen, but determined to attend. My date was June Godkin, an attractive Kingston girl in her first year of Queen's KGH nursing program. I had talked to her on the way to classes and I boarded on a street near her parents' home.

The Arts Formal was our first date and, as it turned out, our last! I had no car to drive June to the dance, so decided to ask an older friend if I could borrow his.

Larry Balfour was a mechanic at the Catherine Street Garage and owned a 1936 Chevrolet that he had adapted to his own needs

1936 Chevrolet sedan in the sales brochure.

as a polio victim who could not use his legs. He had installed a hand throttle and used a crutch against his stomach to depress a bar joining the clutch and brake in such a way that the clutch was depressed before the brake.

I could drive it quite easily, and he lent it to me for the evening. I felt so proud as I drove to June's home, met her parents, escorted her in her long, flimsy, formal dress to the car and so to the gym on Union Street for the dance. Mart Kenny's music was great to dance to and the evening went too quickly.

After 1:00 a.m., in sub-zero weather, we made our way to the cold car to find the battery dead. The '36 Chev was a typical pre-World War II car and nothing much was automatic. The heater was an add-on with its own fan switch not connected to the ignition. The heater fan, which I had neglected to turn off, had drained the battery.

The parked cars along Union Street quickly took off so I got a taxi driver to give the Chev a push to get it started. He saw a puff of smoke from the exhaust as I let out the clutch and presumed the engine had started and so pulled around me and away.

The engine gasped and died. I coasted toward the curb and foolishly put on the brake. Foolishly? The Chev had another glitch I had been told about. The right rear brake shoes sometimes locked on stopping. They did, and I would have to unlock them before hailing another motorist for a push.

There were two ways to unlock the brake. First, put the car in reverse and back up a little (impossible with a dead battery). The alternative: get out and give the frozen wheel a good swift kick. I did. *PSST! Whoosh!* I had kicked the valve stem clean off and down went the tire.

How stupid and inadequate I felt! June was shivering in her taffeta glad rags, the gym was closed, no phone booth near, and not another car in sight.

Wait! A '28 Chev coupe was pulling toward me. I hailed it and it stopped. O frabjous day, callooh, callay! Oh what a sight on a frigid night! The driver was my friend, Clare Kellogg, a theology student who had already delivered his own date to her abode.

His old jalopy had a blow-through manifold heater. Gentleman Clare generously offered to transport my date and June was content to snuggle in beside him.

I sheepishly and apologetically wished June good night and waved goodbye as they pulled away, leaving me to jack up the Chev and put on the spare tire. My friend Larry had the car towed to his garage in the morning and June and I did not date after that!

I cannot remember whether I ever asked her out another time, but coincidentally we did meet again briefly fifty years later. I had stopped by a pioneer cemetery near Plevna, researching my wife's family tree and looking for the name HAWS on the tombstones. There I met two men looking for the name GODKIN. June was the only Godkin I had known and so I mentioned the misadventure with the 1936 Chev.

Startled, one man said, "I am June's husband. She is not feeling well so she stayed in the car, but why don't you say hello to her! And by the way, I am not sorry your first date did not turn out. June and I have been very happy together. I can't wish it had been different!"

I thanked him, spoke briefly to June, and took my leave. So ends my story!

CHAPTER TWENTY-EIGHT

1936 Studebaker Sold Because of a Parking Ticket

Bill Blair was born in 1939 and grew up on Garnock Avenue in the east end of Toronto (he now lives in Uxbridge and is an avid collector of service station memorabilia). Just after turning sixteen, he bought a 1936 Studebaker four-door sedan from Paul Armstrong, a young man who lived only a block away. Paul had bought the low-mileage car from the original owner, an elderly gentleman who took excellent care of it.

Two series of Studebakers were built in 1936: the Dictator, with a flathead six engine and 116-inch wheelbase, and the President, with a flathead straight-8 and 125-inch wheelbase. Advertised features included "automatic hill holder, ribbed cast-iron brake drums, full power muffler, all-silent synchronized transmission, new economizer manifold, metal spring covers, water spray to valve seats, X-frame with box-section sides, and double hydraulic shock absorbers." Independent front suspension was also available on certain models. The four-door sedan in the Dictator series had a "Toronto delivered"

Bill Blair's 1936 Studebaker sedan in 1955 and loaded with lots of accessories.

price of $1212 when you could buy a new 1936 Ford sedan for $891. The larger President sedan would cost you $1755, nearly twice the price of a new Ford.

Bill knew his parents would not be happy with their son buying a car, so he didn't mention it. To keep them in the dark, he parked it in a garage he rented from one of his paper-route customers (Bill delivered the *Toronto Daily Star*). For the next several months his parents were oblivious to Bill's newfound freedom.

Eager to have the snazziest-looking 1936 Studebaker in Toronto, he installed an outside sun visor, fender skirts, whitewall tires, headlight eyebrows, a hood-mounted bug deflector, fog lights, chrome license plate frames, and chrome fender adornments from Canadian Tire.

It was a beautiful riding car. Under the side-opening "butterfly" hood was a flathead 6-cylinder engine with 218 cubic inches cranking out 90 horsepower at 3400 rpm. The transmission was a three-speed with floor-mounted gearshift lever and synchromesh into second and third. Bill's Studebaker was equipped with the optional overdrive which gave him great fuel economy on the highway. It also had the optional "startix" with the starter button under the gas pedal.

During the summer of 1955, Bill enjoyed many pleasant drives to Musselman's Lake north of Toronto. He often visited his uncle, who had a farm north of the lake and frequently dated Miranda, a young lady who lived on the farm across the road. Their paths crossed briefly fifty years later when Bill turned up at her house in Uxbridge to give her an estimate on cleaning her rugs before putting her house up for sale. He did not recognize her, but she recognized him.

Bill's parents discovered he owned the Studebaker when a parking ticket arrived in the mail. Bill's dad was a Toronto police officer and told his son in no uncertain terms to get rid of it. Bill sold it to Norm Charlton on nearby Hogarth Avenue for $50. Norm was buying and selling used cars out of his backyard. By the 1960s, he graduated to a used car lot of his own on Greenwood Avenue, near Gerrard. One of his customers was a young man named Vern Kipp, who bought a 1953 Mercury from Norm, but that's another story.

CHAPTER TWENTY-NINE

1937 Ford Hot Rod Pulled Over by Ottawa Police

Bill MacCallum enjoys reading my "Old Car Detective" column in the Kanata *EMC*. He vividly remembers a car he bought over fifty years ago:

> When I was seventeen in 1957, a friend of mine was in a quandary. Don and his friend Chuck had purchased a genuine hot rod and brought it onto campus at Ashbury College, much to the displeasure of the dean who ordered "that vile thing" off campus. While I was still going to Buckingham High School at the time, I had a part-time job and was able to take the car "off Don's hands" for the princely sum of $50 (all the money I could scrape up at the time).
>
> The original owner had it built by "Young's Speed Shop" (then on Bank Street in Ottawa) in 1952 for $2000 (more than the price of a new Oldsmobile). It

This awesome-looking 1937 Ford coupe was squealing its tires in Ottawa over fifty years ago.

was $400 for the 1937 Ford coupe and $1600 for the mechanical work.

The original 60 hp aluminum block V-8 was replaced with a souped-up '48 Mercury flathead V-8. The block was overbored and fitted with over-sized pistons, the heads were planed to increase compression, and a three-quarter race cam was installed along with twin Holly carburetors on an Edelbrock manifold.

I was told that the original owner had a couple of friends who set up a speed trap (the old two wire variety) on a runway at Rockcliffe Air Base one night, and he put the car over the trap at 137 mph.

I was constantly challenged to drag races, which I usually won. One such race was with a '56 Olds "98".

Bill MacCallum posing with pride alongside his 1937 Ford hot rod.

We were at a light heading west on Wellington Street just in front of the Chateau Laurier. I was beating the Olds when a big burly cop stepped off the sidewalk at the cenotaph and flagged me over. He said he was taking this 'heap' off the road.

An inspection revealed that the car had no emergency brake (with the compression I had, who needs it?), no headlights (I told him I was on my way to CTC to buy fuses), and the mufflers were inadequate. After we talked for a few minutes, he let me go with a $3 fine for disturbing the peace.

The next year (1958), Quebec instituted mandatory insurance for all drivers. Now I was in a quandary, as no insurance company would touch me. My father solved the problem by selling the car when I was out one day. He sold it for $75 (I had turned down $300 two days prior). The last time I saw the car, it was in a race at Lansdowne Park where it got wrecked. What a sad end for such a great car ...

After that car appeared in my "Old Car Detective" column in his local *EMC* paper in March 2008, Bill MacCallum sent me this email: "Hello, Bill: Thank you very much for publishing the story and picture of my '37 Ford coupe. I received a call from a chap in Manotick (south of Ottawa) who said that he remembers the car when it was first built in 1952 and saw it as his dream car."

CHAPTER THIRTY

1937 Ford Hot Rod Pulled Over by Kingston Police

Don Bedore was born in 1935 and grew up in Kingston, Ontario (he now lives in Leamington). As a teenager, he was eager to get a car of his own.

Things got rolling when his friend Charlie O'Connor purchased a 1937 Ford coach for $200 from Patterson Motors at Princess and Regent in the summer of 1953. Charlie brought the car to Don's parents' home where they had a garage workshop in a converted livery stable beside their house on Victoria Street.

Here is where they planned to work wonders with the old Ford, which they claimed "had a lot of potential." Millard & Lumb Iron Works removed all four fenders, which held the running lights. Also removed were the bumpers and running boards. With the car now stripped of all "unnecessary" parts, it began to look like a real hot rod.

Everything was going according to plan until one evening when Don drove Charlie home in the fenderless Ford. A block from home,

Don Bedore behind the wheel of his 1937 "fenderless" Ford in Kingston, Ontario, in 1953. He drove it like this, then sold it to a scrapyard for $20.

he was pulled over by a police officer for having no lights. Don pleaded with him that everything was okay because "my dash lights are still working." The officer smiled as he gave Don a ticket for improper lights.

Less than a week later, Don got a phone call from J.T. Truaisch, chief of police. In a stern voice the chief demanded: "What's going on with you and Charlie and that car? Get down to the station right now!" Don jumped onto his old CCM bicycle and pedalled the three miles downtown with his heart beating faster than his legs were moving. Charlie was already there. The chief told them that Charlie's mother had found out about the car and if Charlie didn't get rid of it, his job as chief was on the line.

The chief told Don and Charlie, "If this car is out of Charlie's name, I'll look after the ticket" (which was still unpaid). Don had saved $75 from his job at Loblaws stacking shelves for fifty cents an hour and offered all of it to Charlie. And that's how Don came to purchase his first car.

With no money left to fix it up, it sat outside over the next winter. When spring came, Don discovered the block and rad were cracked, as the car had not been winterized. He sold it to an auto wrecker for $20. To this day he feels he should have paid the ticket instead! Since then, Don Bedore has owned forty-two cars, including a 1940 Ford convertible he bought in running condition for $90 soon after saying goodbye to the 1937, but that's another story.

The 1937 Ford boasted several advances for its day, including headlights blended into the front fenders. But with his front fenders gone, this advance was of no concern to young Don Bedore.

CHAPTER THIRTY-ONE

1938 Ford: "Not Perfect, But It was a Convertible!"

*T*he late Jack McLeod enjoyed reading my "Old Car Detective" column in the Essex Free Press. He remembered a convertible he bought in Windsor, Ontario, nearly sixty years ago.

I was driving home from work one day when I saw a 1938 Ford convertible sitting on a used car lot. I had to stop and take a look. I walked around it and it looked a little rough, but when you're young, it was springtime, it was a convertible, and I had never owned one before.

Front view of 1938 Ford convertible photographed by the "Old Car Detective" at a car show in Hershey, Pennsylvania. Ford offered four versions of a convertible in 1938: a two-door convertible with rumble seat, a two-door club convertible with back seat under the top and no rumble seat, a four-door convertible with roll-up windows, and a four-door phaeton with side curtains.

I was talking myself into buying this car before I knew what they were asking for it. The salesman had the usual spiel as to how rare it was, how good it was, and how lucky I was to be one of the first to even view this marvellous car. I had to have it. I took it for a short drive around the block and all the things I noticed were wrong with it didn't even register in my mind. It was a convertible, don't forget.

Well, that car proved to be "something else." When you opened the door, it dropped about three inches, but some convertibles do that. They tried to mask the smell of the oil-burning engine with toilet deodorant. It took two people to force the top down. The clutch chattered so bad, it almost shook the car apart. The shimmy at thirty miles an hour almost shook the steering wheel off. It burned so much oil, you had to drive with the windows down, but that wasn't so bad. It was a convertible, you know.

The floor had numerous holes, the gearshift lever seemed to go anywhere but where you wanted it, the steering wheel almost felt like it wasn't connected to anything, and it took a lot of steering to keep the car on the road. I picked up my new girlfriend to show her my convertible, but after a short ride I don't think she was impressed. The car was a nightmare.

I put it up for sale at the side of the road. Along came a fellow from Amherstburg about my age and driving a 1938 Chev two-door. Guess what? He did the same thing as I did, he fell in love with that 1938 Ford convertible. I told him it had lots of things wrong with it, but you know the old saying: "Love is blind." In no time we made a deal. He drove away in the 1938 Ford convertible and I fell in love with his 1938 Chev.

CHAPTER THIRTY-TWO

1938 Pontiac Stops for Gas in Saskatchewan

F ellow old car enthusiast Rickard Busse of Calgary, Alberta, recently sent me the photo you see here of his dad, Henry R. Busse (1918–1985), standing between two Imperial Oil clear-vision, gravity-feed gas pumps at Manitou Beach, Saskatchewan, around 1938. Mr. Busse was about twenty years old at the time. Manitou is the only inland salt-water lake in Canada. The boat house did oil changes and tune-ups and rented rowboats and outboards.

The boat house was next to Danceland with a five-thousand-square-foot hardwood floor mounted on bales of horsehair. The floor moved up and down as the people danced. When the dance ended at midnight, Richard Busse's dad opened the boat house and rented every boat!

The car at the gas pumps is a new (or nearly new) 1938 Pontiac coach. When its tank got filled, the amount charged was calculated by how far down the level of gas was reduced on the clear-vision gas

pump. Many of these pumps were filled by hand-pumping the gas up from underground containers.

For 1938, Pontiac was available in three series: the low-priced 2500 Special, the medium-priced 2600 Deluxe, and the top-of-the-line Deluxe Eight. Pontiac's selling features for 1938 included a "V-type windshield, safety glass, Fisher Unisteel Turret Top (an all-steel roof), no-draft ventilation, double-action shock absorbers, and a body completely insulated against noise, heat, and cold."

The low- and medium-priced Pontiacs were built by GM of Canada in Oshawa and Regina and employed the 1938 Chevrolet overhead-valve six cylinder engine. It's a safe bet that the car in the photo was built in Regina. The least-expensive 1938 Pontiac was the two-passenger business coupe with a factory retail price of $895. The most expensive 1938 Pontiac in Canada was the Deluxe Eight six-passenger convertible sedan at $1859. The two-door Pontiac in the photo is probably a 2500 Special with a factory retail price of $940.

If you look closely at the right front fender of that car, you will see an accessory not seen anymore: a fender guide. Because of the height of the hood, the driver cannot see the right front fender. The fender guide reduced the risk of scratches or dents on the body and scuff marks on whitewall tires if you had them.

Old Autos columnist Alvin Shier is compiling a Canadian Pontiac Registry and now has on file over six hundred Pontiacs built in Canada since 1926. If you own a Canadian-built Pontiac and wish to add it to the Registry, write to Alvin Shier, 844 Lawrence Grassi Ridge, Canmore, Alberta, T1W 2Y6.

CHAPTER THIRTY-THREE

1939 Pontiac Business Coupe: Sold It Once and Bought It Twice

Back in 1970, Ken Lalonde of Tilbury, Ontario, was married for a couple of years with a good job, a new car, and a house with a garage. That's when the bug hit him to find an old car.

On a bright Saturday in September, my wife and I began driving around looking for one. Just ten miles out of Tilbury beside Meyers' auto wreckers and gas station, I spotted a beat-up old car. It was, as they say, "nice from far, but far from good." For $100, I became the proud owner of a 1939 Pontiac business coupe.

My friend Bert Reaume helped me bring it home with a tow rope around his rear bumper and my front axle. I steered while sitting on a tomato basket and I

Ken Lalonde's 1939 Pontiac business coupe the second time around.

could see the pavement passing under me. When we reached home, my dad asked: "What are you going to do with that?" And I said: "We're going to fix her up, Pop."

Ken had no idea how much work was ahead of him, but his dad did. He was a metal finisher at Ford Motor Company and also worked weekends at Ken's uncle's body shop. Friends loaned him their tools and torches, and Dad taught Ken how to braze and weld with steel coat hangers. He also taught him the mechanics of the car, and most of all he taught him patience.

"By next spring," recalls Ken, "I was on the road with a new burgundy finish, black naugahyde bucket seats, and a 283 Chevy under the hood. The car was finished two days before the local July 1 parade. Five years later, and with a growing family, I reluctantly sold it."

The years rolled by and Ken retired. Around this time, someone told him of an old coupe at a body shop two blocks from where he used to work. He called the shop and the owner said he had a 1939 Pontiac coupe for sale. He had owned it for twenty years. Could it be the same car? It was! Ken saw it tucked away in a corner of the shop, half painted, half primed, and with parts taken off. He bought it, and after some reassembly, was able to drive it home, right past the Meyers garage on old Hwy. 2.

It's now bright red with a red-and-white interior, highly polished ET rims, and the 283 Chev V8 still under the hood. I met Ken and his Pontiac at the Belle River Classic Car Show on July 16 and … WOW! WHAT A CAR!

CHAPTER THIRTY-FOUR

1940 Chrysler Convertible Built Same Year Walter Chrysler Died

Around 1951, Jack Brigden purchased a 1940 Chrysler convertible from Elmer Queen's Chrysler-Plymouth Motor Sales in Essex, Ontario, for approximately $1400 (Elmer Queen was mayor of Essex at that time). It was grey with fenders molded to the body, blue fender skirts, a blue plastic after-market sun visor, fog lights, a grille guard, and snap-on metal whitewalls that were popular in the years after the war.

Jack's convertible was just about the snazziest car in town, and the only one of its kind around here back then. The car was rare even when new because most new car buyers in Canada in 1940 chose coupes or sedans. A convertible was a real extravagance in 1940, especially considering our country was at war.

Jack's Chrysler was built the same year that Walter P. Chrysler died — at age sixty-five. Chrysler was born in 1875 and grew up in Iowa.

Here is Jack Brigden's 1940 Chrysler convertible with the old Essex post office in the background.

He fell in love with automobiles while attending a car show in Chicago soon after the turn of the last century. The car that caught his eye was a white Locomobile with red leather upholstery. The price tag was $5000 and even though Mr. Chrysler had only $700 in cash, his bank back home loaned him $4300 so he could buy the car. He had it shipped by rail to his farm because he did not know how to drive. As soon as it got there, he rolled it into the barn and took it all apart. He did this several times because he wanted to know how it was made. In 1925, he used the faltering Maxwell Company to launch the Chrysler Corporation, and three years later bought the Dodge Company. In that same year of 1928, he also introduced the Plymouth and DeSoto. Now people began referring to General Motors, Ford, and Chrysler as the "Big Three."

The previous owner of Jack's convertible (who was not necessarily the first owner) was Smitty of Smitty's Texaco station on Ouellette Avenue in Windsor. He traded it in at Queen's Motor Sales on a late model car and that's how Jack had the opportunity to buy it. He owned it for at least four years and never had a problem with it, except on the night he went to the movie theatre in Leamington with some friends, then had to hurry back to Essex to meet his wife getting off work at midnight. He drove the car pretty hard to get there on time, and when he stopped the car at her place of work with two minutes to spare, the right front end dropped down and the right front wheel fell flat on the road.

That's when Jack discovered the car had been in an accident before he bought it. Luckily, his dad, Bill Brigden, operated a Shell service station and Jack arranged with Chester Gunning to tow his car to his dad's shop, where it was repaired. Jack's dad was well-known in the Essex area. He operated his service station in that town for some forty years.

Jack was born in Essex in 1930 and grew up around all the cars we wish we owned today. He bought his first car through his dad — a 1932 Ford Model B coupe in tip-top shape. It was a three-window coupe with suicide doors. He purchased his first new car in 1956 — a Pontiac Laurentian with all the options from Dumouchelle Motors in Essex.

Jack has owned many other cars over the years, but his 1940 Chrysler convertible still occupies a special place in his heart. One look at the photo you see here brings all those great memories back again.

CHAPTER THIRTY-FIVE

Al "Fireball" Rouhinen's Cool 1940 Ford Coupe

A l Rouhinen has always been crazy about cars. When he was fifteen and living in the east end of Toronto, he hot-wired his dad's 1951 Meteor with cigarette paper and took it out for a spin. He smashed the front end against two cedar fence posts and had to pay for the damage with money earned on his paper route.

Al's first car that actually ran was a 1940 Ford coupe that he bought for $100. It was powered by a 1953 Mercury flathead and the body was in red primer. He was risking a change of address by buying the '40 because his dad had told him he would be thrown out of the house if he bought a car. Al asked Martti Leivo's parents if he could sleep in their basement, then he drove the '40 home and showed it to his dad. Luckily, his dad had owned a 1941 Studebaker just before Al was born and so a '40 Ford was okay. Al was allowed to keep it.

Martti's dad had owned a 1948 Plymouth years earlier. It was now long gone, but the radio was still in the Leivo basement. It ended up slung under the dash of Al's 1940 coupe and it blasted away with all the latest rock 'n' roll.

In June 1960, young Al Rouhinen draped himself across the front fender of his tough-looking 1940 Ford coupe with naked red rims and Canadian Tire portawalls — the perfect car for a nineteen-year-old hot rodder over fifty years ago. For several years Al operated Draggin' Unlimited, a speed equipment store at St. Clair and O'Connor in the east end of Toronto. He and his wife often dropped into the store after hours and danced to all their favourite rock 'n' roll tunes.

Al and Martti drove the '40 to Detroit on the Labour Day weekend in 1960 to attend the National Drags at the Detroit Dragway at Sibley and Dix. A fellow from New Mexico was there with a louver press set up right beside the drag strip. Al couldn't resist, and for only ten cents apiece, his hood was stamped with 106 louvers. His 1940 Ford coupe now looked very intimidating. But the louvers were a nuisance on rainy days. Water would get into the engine and make it hard to start.

Hungry for more horsepower, Al picked up a "283" small block Chevy from a wrecking yard, then took it to an engine shop in the east end of Toronto where it was machined to perfection. But before the engine was ready for the road, Al sold his 1940 Ford coupe and the engine ended up in a 1955 Chev that Al purchased from Humberview Motors in the west end of Toronto in 1962. Another story ...

Someone reading this story might be the person who bought that 1940 Ford coupe from "Fireball" Rouhinen half a century ago, and that could bring us yet another story!

CHAPTER THIRTY-SIX

Almost a Movie Star: My 1940 McLaughlin-Buick Coupe

*F*rom time to time, readers of my "Old Car Detective" weekly column
have asked me to write a story about an old car I have owned. Here is one
of those stories.

On November 23, 1939, a farmer named Milt Mason bought a new
1940 McLaughlin-Buick Super coupe for $1528 from Ray Young, the
Pontiac-Buick dealer in my hometown of Leamington, Ontario. The
car was a beautiful sky blue and under the hood was Buick's legendary
straight-8 overhead-valve engine with 248 cubic inches producing 107
horsepower.

During the 1940s, Mr. Mason drove the car to Florida at least twice,
and gave it excellent care. When he traded it in on a new Buick in 1951

*This photo of my 1940 McLaughlin-Buick Super coupe was taken around 1984 in Toronto soon after I purchased
a pair of personalized "SHERK" license plates.*

at Ray Young's dealership, the car was still in showroom condition. A Greyhound bus driver named Glenn Fox from Windsor purchased the car for $1100 and gave it excellent care for the next seven years.

In June 1958, the 1940 Buick was once again traded it Ray Young's dealership in favour of a new Vauxhall. The 1940 Buick had now gone 64,364 miles and still looked showroom-fresh. Ray Young put it up for sale for $550.

Two teenage brothers were working for Ray Young that summer. My older brother, John Sherk, was in the parts department and I was washing the used cars. I had just turned sixteen, John was eighteen, and our parents suggested we look for a good used car for ourselves. We bought the 1940 Buick for $500. It was in mint condition.

At the end of the summer, we drove the 1940 Buick to our home in Toronto, where John and I attended high school. In October 1959, we put our car on display at the first Fort York Armoury Autorama, where our car was surrounded by a dazzling array of Toronto hot rods and customized cars. Three months later, we displayed the car again, this time at the first Speed Sport show in January 1960, where the car earned a trophy for FIRST IN CLASS RESTORED.

By 1964, we were living in Toronto permanently and John bought a new 1964 Corvair Monza Spyder convertible, then signed his half of the 1940 Buick over to me. Seven years later, in 1971, I drove our 1940 McLaughlin-Buick through the circular driveway of the Parkwood estate in Oshawa, along with fifty other McLaughlin-Buicks, to celebrate Colonel Sam McLaughlin's hundredth birthday. He brought General Motors to Canada in 1918.

Also in 1971, I drove it to Hart House on the University of Toronto Campus in downtown Toronto for the shooting of a Warner Bros. movie *Class of '44*. Several vintage cars (including mine!) were parked in front of the camera. When the shooting began, I was convinced my car was well on the way to becoming a movie star with contracts pouring in for more movies.

The movie came out a year later and our family went to see it. When my car appeared on the screen, I jumped up and shouted: "That's my car!" The scene switched even before I finished getting the words out.

All that we saw was my front fender and it was on the screen for less than two seconds.

Our 1940 McLaughlin-Buick Super coupe stayed in the Sherk family for thirty years and is now owned by a man in Alliston, Ontario. It's still a good car and it's still on the road, but has yet to appear in another movie.

CHAPTER THIRTY-SEVEN

Teenager Photographs Cadillac Convertible in Alberta in 1946

At age thirteen, Ed Wong snapped this photo of a 1941 Cadillac convertible sedan that took him and his family on a sight-seeing tour from Banff to Lake Louise in Alberta in 1946. Through the windshield, you can see another Cadillac convertible parked behind. Brewster Bus Lines reportedly bought twelve of these rare convertible sedans brand new.

Ed Wong, a vintage car enthusiast now living in Toronto, grew up in Olds, Alberta. He was thirteen in the summer of 1946 when he and his parents boarded a train to Calgary and then to Banff, where they rented a taxi for a drive to Lake Louise.

That taxi was a very rare 1941 Cadillac four-door convertible, one of only four hundred built that year. Brewster Bus Lines in Banff reportedly owned twelve of them. The photo shown here was taken by young Ed and shows the car they rented with its top down. A second 1941 Cadillac four-door convertible with its top up and parked behind can be seen through the windshield. Their uniformed driver is standing beside the car they rode in and Cascade Mountain is faintly visible in the background.

Cadillacs for 1941 were powered by a flathead V-8 engine cranking out 150 hp at 3400 rpm from 346 cubic inches. The Series 62 four-door convertible (also called a "convertible sedan") rode on a wheelbase of 126 inches and weighed 4230 pounds. Interiors were finished in genuine leather.

Sometime after the Wong family visited Banff, Brewster Bus Lines sold off their twelve 1941 Cadillac convertible sedans to make room for more modern vehicles. Do any of the twelve still exist?

I asked that question of Ed Wong. He remembers seeing a 1941 Cadillac four-door convertible in a wrecking yard in Wetaskawin, Alberta, in the 1960s. The yard was owned by the brother of Stan Reynolds, who collected an enormous number of antique cars, many of which are now on display in the large car museum that Wetaskawin is now famous for. I phoned the Reynolds museum while I was working on this book and learned that they do not have one of these Cadillacs in their vast collection. The 1941 Cadillac that Ed Wong saw in the wrecking yard some forty years ago might have come from the Brewster Bus Lines fleet of twelve. And perhaps someone rescued it and restored it.

In the 1970s, Kent Weale of Port Credit, Ontario, visited the late Slim Jenns of 100 Mile House in British Columbia. Slim had a collection of ten or so vintage automobiles, and a dark gray 1941 Cadillac four-door convertible in excellent condition was among them. Perhaps this car also may have come from the Brewster fleet.

Meanwhile, back in Olds, ten years after the visit to Banff, Ed Wong was twenty-three and driving a customized coral-and-cream 1952 Oldsmobile two-door hardtop with 1954 Buick headlight rims and 1955 Packard tail lights. Some of the older residents of Olds probably still remember that car. Today, Ed is the proud owner of two 1947 Chrysler Town and Country wood-bodied convertibles, which he has restored. But he still thinks back to that black 1941 Cadillac convertible sedan he photographed so long ago.

CHAPTER THIRTY-EIGHT

1941 Mercury Convertible from South America to Newfoundland

Ed Bannister's yellow 1941 Mercury convertible in Corner Brook, Newfoundland.

Gord Harsell's street-rodded 1941 Mercury convertible in Warkworth, Ontario.

Since the 1970s, I have been a frequent visitor to Fawcett Motors in Whitby, Ontario, where vintage cars are bought, sold, and restored. The late Ron Fawcett operated the business for many years, and it is now in the capable hands of his son, Peter Fawcett, and Peter's business partner, Art Carty.

I dropped in one day around 1990 and saw a very interesting car in their showroom: an unrestored, but otherwise complete, 1941 Mercury convertible that had just arrived from South America. It was right-hand-drive and the speedometer was in kilometres. The car was sold to Richard Maidman of Grand Falls, Newfoundland, who proceeded to restore the car and changed the colour from red to yellow. Unfortunately, he developed cancer and only rode in the car a couple of times before he passed away.

Another member of the family dismantled the car with the intention of restoring it again. It remained apart until 2003 when it was purchased by Ed Bannister of Corner Brook, Newfoundland. The car has been partially reassembled and Ed hopes to have it back on the road some day.

Ed's wife worked in the office of the local high school (Templeton Collegiate) for many years. It has now been replaced by a larger school, Templeton Academy, that houses both elementary and secondary school students. Ed and a partner purchased the old high school and now store vintage cars in there for people in the area who need winter storage. His 1941 Mercury convertible is also stored in there.

Gord Harsell of Warkworth, Ontario, put me in touch with Ed Bannnister. Gord owned a 1941 Mercury convertible when he was a teenager living in southern Ontario in the 1950s. That car is long gone (he found the hood years later), but Gord today owns *two* 1941 Mercury convertibles: one restored to original and the other a street rod with a Corvette drive train.

But Gord's enthusiasm for 1941 Mercury convertibles is not confined to the two he owns. For several years now, he has been compiling a worldwide registry of 1941 Mercury convertibles to see how many still exist and to provide a means whereby the owners of these cars can contact one another to assist with restorations.

Gord has found several of these cars in the United States and others as far away as South America and New Zealand. He is currently constructing a 1941 Mercury Ute (short for "utility" vehicle) similar to the Fords manufactured in Australia beginning in 1947. The Ford Motor Company never built a 1941 Mercury Ute, and Gord's will be the first! For more information, Gord Harsell can be reached at *fragor@sympatico.ca*.

CHAPTER THIRTY-NINE

1941 Oldsmobile Convertible in Quebec Junkyard

Dave Tafel lives today in Orleans, Ontario, and reads my column in the local *EMC* paper. He was born in 1941 and still remembers the car he and some friends almost purchased over half a century ago.

> When I was fifteen or sixteen, we lived in Trois-Rivières, Quebec, and I ran with a crowd that was slightly older … late teens! We wanted to build the hottest hot rod around and we found a yellow 1941 Olds convertible with four wide whitewall tires sitting in a junkyard on the east side of the main road between Shawinigan and Trois-Rivières, just a bit north of St. Louis de France (Route 157).
>
> The asking price was a bit steep, probably because it was equipped with Hydra-Matic (one of the first automatic transmissions). When it came to the point of purchase, we looked it over and found that the frame was rotted beyond repair so we didn't buy it. None of

1941 Oldsmobile Special convertible coupe in the sales brochure.

us had the garage, tools, or expertise to complete the job, anyway.

It would have become a money pit and we really didn't have lots of bucks, either. The original plan was to drop an Olds Rocket V-8 (1950 vintage) into it and marry that to a 1937 Cadillac or LaSalle floor-shift tranny, which the little hot rod magazines told us was strong and would maybe stand up to some abuse.

Anyway, the dream went into the dustbin and I ended up with the service manuals for the 1941 Olds and 1937 Cadillac-LaSalle. Gawd only knows where they came from. I've stored them with my old *Hot Rod* magazines all these years. The experience was probably the impetus for me to sign up for Mechanical Engineering at the University of New Brunswick several years later.

If Dave and the boys had bought the 1941 Olds convertible with the intention of replacing the frame with one from a sedan, they would have been asking for trouble. Page twelve of the 1941 Olds manual states that convertibles had a stronger-than-normal frame because open cars lack the rigidity of a closed body. They would have had to find another 1941 Olds convertible with a solid frame, an almost impossible task since convertibles built in 1941were rare in wartime Canada.

He can't remember if the Olds convertible in the junkyard was a two-door or four-door convertible. Both body styles were available that year, with the four-door convertible being rare even when new and almost impossible to find today. I saw one at a car show in Michigan in 1968 and have not seen one since.

Dave and I hope this story will be reprinted in the local papers in the Trois-Rivières and Shawinigan area. Someone living there today might remember the yellow 1941 Olds convertible in the local junkyard and who owned it when it was on the road. If something turns up, you'll read all about it in my next book, where we bring old cars back to life.

CHAPTER FORTY

His 1942 Ford Smoked So Bad, No One Would Ride with Him

W*ith the outbreak of World War II, the auto industry in North America began turning out tanks, planes, jeeps, and guns. Civilian production of automobiles ended in February 1942 and no new cars were built for the next three years. The 1942 model year was short-lived, making those cars rare when new and very scarce today.*

Ron Lepine of Kanata, Ontario, owned a 1942 Ford coupe many years ago.

It was my first car and I bought it for $50 from my neighbour. The radiator leaked and the rear end dripped oil. Every time I went anywhere, I had to fill the rad with water and carry a five-gallon pail full of water for the trip back home. Finally, I got enough money to buy a used rad for $14. I tightened the bolts on the rear end and the leak stopped.

1942 Ford six-passenger sedan coupe in the sales brochure ("the ideal car for small families"). The 1942 Fords were available in a range of colours: Florentine Blue, Newcastle Gray, Niles Blue-Green, Fathom Blue, Moselle Maroon, and Black.

A week later, I took a trip to the Adirondacks in New York and drove up Whiteface Mountain. The car overheated going up those long steep hills and I had to stop at every switchback to let the motor cool down. On the way back down, I broke a rear spring and had to put a flat rock on the axle housing to keep the tire from rubbing on the fender. It was a bumpy ride and I had to stop and replace the rock several times. I finally got home and replaced the spring with a used one from a wrecker.

One day while out fishing in the woods, I got stuck and broke an axle. I had to get towed home and it took a couple of weeks to find another axle.

All summer the car ran good, but driving in the winter was not easy. The heater could hardly keep up with the cold air blowing through the rust holes in the floor and around the doors. Where I lived was very cold, in the minus 30–40 [Celsius] range. With no block heater, I had to drain the oil into an old dish pan and put it behind the wood stove in the kitchen. In the morning, I would pour the warm oil back into the engine and that's how I got it to start.

I drove the car for about two years until it broke a couple of oil rings on the flathead V8 engine and smoked so bad that no one would ride with me. I finally drove it to a wrecking yard and got $35 for it. I sure miss my first car even though it had ripped seats, a poor heater, and a noisy rear end. I had many good times driving my first car.

CHAPTER FORTY-ONE

1942 Ford Convertible Found in a Swamp

Art Parliament of Belleville, Ontario, is the proud owner of a very rare car — a 1942 Ford convertible. Production of civilian automobiles ended in February 1942 because of the Second World War and only 2,920 Ford convertibles were built for that model year. Contrast that with 31,589 Ford convertibles built for the 1941 model year. The 1942 Mercury convertible was even more rare than the Ford, with only 956 produced.

Several years ago, a friend of Art's was deer-hunting in the bush north of Kingston when he found the remains of a black 1942 Ford convertible in a swamp. It had apparently been there for quite some time. The interior contained a foot of silt and some kids had built a fire inside the car to keep warm while skating on a pond. Art located the owner of the property, then purchased the car, and brought it home.

Art Parliament poses with pride alongside his cool ride, a 1942 Ford convertible with 1947 Ford front-end sheet metal and modern state-of-the-art running gear.

"What am I getting into?" Art wondered as he looked at the pitiful remains of the car over the next two years. Finally deciding to forge ahead, he had the body sandblasted. Several coats of paint came off as it was taken down to bare metal, and the body turned out to be surprisingly solid. The car was worthy of being brought back to life.

The top mechanism was completely missing. Art and his friend Roy Robertson of Peterborough headed to Hershey, Pennsylvania, to the big annual antique car swap meet hosted by the AACA (Antique Automobile Club of America) in search of a new folding top for his car. For three days, they trudged through endless fields of cars and parts without finding what they were looking for. When they reached the last row, Art said he was too tired to go on. Roy persuaded him to continue and that's where they found a folding top to fit his car.

Art rebuilt the original 1942 Ford frame and attached a Nova front clip for better handling. The engine compartment now houses a 350 fuel-injected small block Chevrolet V-8 connected to a 700 R4 automatic transmission and 9-inch Ford rear end. The original 1942 Ford engine had 221 cubic inches with 90 horsepower and the transmission was a three-speed column shift.

To update the look of his 1942 Ford convertible, Art visited Hershey again and bought the 1947 Ford front sheet metal, which is now on his car (it is now registered as a '47). The red and black colour scheme is dazzling, and the door handles and trunk handle have been shaved and replaced with electric doors and trunk. The car is a pleasure to drive and is often seen at cruise nights and car shows in eastern Ontario. We wish Art Parliament many more years of happy motoring with his 1942 Ford reborn as a '47.

CHAPTER FORTY-TWO

No New Cars for Three Years

In February 1942, civilian production of automobiles came to an end because of the Second World War. Bob Chapman was a teenager at the time and worked as a "ramper." He drove cars up and down the ramps at Ontario Automobile, a large Chrysler-Plymouth dealership on Bay Street in downtown Toronto. When no more new cars were available, dozens of them were taken from that dealership and stored in an arena at the north end of the city for emergency use during the war, and no one knew how long the war would last. "We parked those cars door handle to door handle," recalls Chapman many years later. "And the clutch pedals were blocked in the down position to keep them from seizing up." The roof collapsed during a big snowstorm in 1944 and several of the cars were damaged. Bob's father clipped that story out of the daily paper and sent it to Bob overseas in Europe, where he served until the end of the war. He carried that clipping in his knapsack until war's end and he still has it to this day.

With new cars no longer available, dealerships had to rely on their stock of used cars to stay in business. General Motors of Canada published a 324-page 1942 *Used Car Sales Handbook* of Features for all its dealers across Canada, listing all domestic makes from 1935 to 1941 in alphabetical order from Auburn to Willys. A full page was devoted to each make and year with a wealth of information on each car, including engine specifications, wheelbase, tires, brakes, body, special features, Canadian prices when new, and manufacturer's outstanding selling points (e.g. 1938 DeSoto: 1. Riding Comfort. 2. Operating Economy. 3. Beauty. 4. Roominess. 5. Safety."). The first page of the handbook says: "The FACTS and FEATURES that SOLD THEM NEW WILL SELL THEM NOW if you will use this information in your ADVERTISING COPY and SALES TALKS DAILY."

Gas rationing became a fact of everyday life in Canada during the war because of the need to conserve gasoline and rubber. In Ontario, because of the shortage of metal, no front license plates were issued from 1943 until 1947. No plates at all were available in 1944. Motorists had to purchase a blue sticker and display it in the lower passenger side of the windshield. You can see one of those stickers in the windshield of the 1940 Mercury two-door sedan photographed here in the gravel driveway of a home in North Toronto in the summer of 1944 while the owner and his two sons wash the car. The little two-year-old boy being held up by his dad is the author of this book.

PART TWO: 1946 to 1965

N ew cars finally appeared in the fall of 1945, and they were facelifted versions of the cars built in 1942. Demand was so great after the Second World War that some people had their names on waiting lists at the local dealership for a year or more. And some of the new cars were missing some parts. Earl Domm purchased a new 1946 Hudson sedan from Century Motors on Yonge Street in Toronto. It had wooden bumpers on the front and rear, no back seat, and no plastic knob on the end of the gearshift lever. All these parts were on back order and would be installed on the car when they became available. On trips to the Domm family cottage on Lake Simcoe, Earl and Mabel's two children sat in the back seat on folding lawn chairs.

The Studebaker Corporation of South Bend, Indiana, was the first car manufacturer to bring out a new model after the war, and the new 1947 Studebaker arrived in the spring of 1946. The company boasted of being "first by far with a postwar car." That was ironic because Studebaker built its last car in 1966, squeezed out by competition from the Big Three. Packard, Hudson, Nash, and Kaiser disappeared even earlier. They were all gone by the end of the 1950s.

By 1949, all car companies had their new postwar models in the showrooms and they created a sensation with their fresh new styling. The horsepower race started this year with both Oldsmobile and Cadillac arriving with powerful overhead-valve V-8 engines. By the early 1950s, even Chevrolet, Ford, and Plymouth in the low-priced field were available with automatic transmissions and hardtops that eliminated the B-pillar (a style that has now largely disappeared).

Annual styling changes were eagerly anticipated by a car-crazy public wallowing in the newfound prosperity of the 1950s and early 1960s. Horsepower ratings climbed steadily with new cars while teenagers across the country bought older cars and souped them up.

It was an exciting time to get your driver's licence, and I suspect that many of the people reading this book right now got their licence during those "Baby Boom" years from 1946 to 1965.

CHAPTER FORTY-THREE

1946 Buick with Blowtorch Heater

Ralph Arbeau of Pine Glen, New Brunswick, was fifteen years old in 1957 when he bought his first car, a 1947 Chevrolet sedan, for $100. He then traded that car for a 1951 Ford convertible and then traded the Ford for a 1946 Buick four-door sedan.

The Buick had a big straight-8 engine with a three-speed standard transmission with gearshift on the steering column ("three on the tree" as we used to say). Ralph was living in Burnt Church, New Brunswick, at the time and did not have much money for repairs. If something broke on the Buick, it stayed that way as long as the car kept running.

Back then, many Buicks had an auxiliary heater under the passenger side of the front seat for the benefit of rear-seat passengers.

1946 Buick Super four-door sedan in the sales brochure. Note the big sweeping "airfoil" front fenders that sweep all the way back to the rear fenders, giving these new Buicks a long and low look not matched by any other new cars in 1946. The sales brochure sings the praises of this new Buick: "It's big ... it's beautiful ... it's Buick! No car of ordinary merit would do for the 1946 Buick. We present them proudly as cars not matched anywhere in these times for every-inch goodness. You will drive them proudly for many long and satisfying years to come."

The sales brochure also sings the praises of the Buick Fireball straight eight engine: "There is the valve-in-head principle with the Dynaflash combustion chamber which rolls the fuel into a power-packed charge, squeezes it into a flattened ball so that it lets go with a super-stout wallop.... Yes, this Buick Fireball straight-eight for 1946 is a great engine and made to closer tolerances than an Aircraft Engine."

Ralph's Buick had this deluxe feature, but it was not working properly. This became a problem on a particularly cold Saturday night when Ralph and a couple of friends were taking their dates to a restaurant.

To offset the lack of heat, they placed a blowtorch filled with gas on the floor of the back seat and then picked up the girls and headed for the restaurant. Ralph remembers the evening as if it were yesterday:

> Because it was late in the evening, it was very dark in the car. When we got to the restaurant and walked in, everyone inside started looking at us and laughing. We did not realize that our faces were all black from the soot from the blowtorch. Needless to say, the girls were not impressed.
>
> Also, the wiper cable broke one day, so when it rained we ran a string through the vent windows to the wiper arms. When we drove, we had to pull on each end of the string. Don't think that would pass a safety check today.
>
> I drove that old Buick until I turned seventeen and moved to Toronto. I left the Buick with my foster parents as they had paid my train fare to Ontario. They drove the Buick for a short time, then parked it with other old cars in a field. I came back a year later for a vacation and the old Buick was still in the field minus a few windows broken by local children. A few years later all the old cars, including my Buick, were hauled away for scrap.
>
> I moved back to New Brunswick in 1980. I wish I had taken a picture of that old Buick. It was a lot of fun. Good thing gas was only 30 cents a gallon.

CHAPTER FORTY-FOUR

He Drove His 1946 Ford Coupe to See Elvis

B ob Lindsay lives today in Hamilton, Ontario. His first car took him and his friends to see the King of Rock 'n' Roll over fifty years ago.

My first car was a 1946 Ford five-passenger coupe. We had moved from the farm at Caistor Centre in the Niagara Peninsula and I was working at the John Inglis washing-machine plant in Toronto at the time. At a car lot on Danforth Avenue in Toronto near where I lived, I had the option of purchasing a Lincoln Continental V-12 coupe or a 1946 Ford five-passenger coupe with a 1952 Ford flathead engine. The Lincoln would not start, so I took the Ford. I paid $400 for it in 1956 and financed it through Niagara Finance at $28 a month shortly before moving back to Caistor Centre.

Bob Lindsay took this picture of his 1946 Ford five-passenger coupe in the late 1950s. So great was the demand for new cars after the war that Ford kept almost exactly the same styling for three consecutive model years (1946–1948). The rectangular parking lights above the grille on Bob Lindsay's coupe appeared on all 1946 models and the early 1947s (until all those parts were used up, in keeping with Henry Ford's thrifty policy of not throwing anything useful away). The rest of the 1947s and all the 1948s had round parking lights below the headlights. Bob Lindsay eventually traded his 1946 Ford coupe for a 1953 Mercury sedan, but that's another story ...

This car was built just after the war with what seemed like the same heavy steel they built war vehicles from. Gas at that time was only 25–27 cents a gallon. I had no way of telling what kind of mileage per gallon I was getting because the speedometer did not work. I used about six dollars a week in fuel while driving to work at Day & Campbell in Hamilton. Back then, with no credit cards, you only drove as much as the money in your pocket allowed.

I have seen only two 1946 Ford coupes in recent years. One in Florida was completely rebuilt with modern suspension and a high powered engine, and was for sale for $28,000 (it was a beauty and I wish I had the money). The second, in Port Dover, Ontario, was totally rebuilt as original and was the exact model and colour as mine. It was beautiful and "Not For Sale." I owned my 1946 Ford for three years and the most memorable time was when I drove to Toronto with my Caistor Centre friends to see Elvis Presley on April 2, 1957 at Maple Leaf Gardens."

I, too (the future Old Car Detective), was at the Gardens on April 2, 1957. Bob Lindsay and I may have walked past each other while trying to find a seat on the one and only night that Elvis came to Toronto. He belted out all his greatest songs including *Heartbreak Hotel, Hound Dog, Don't Be Cruel*, and the title song from his first movie released just a few months earlier, *Love Me Tender*. It was almost impossible to hear him because his fans (including me) screamed nonstop!

He then went to Ottawa and wanted to stay at the Chateau Laurier, but was refused accommodation because the hotel thought his fans would wreck the place. On January 8, 2010, he would have turned seventy-five.

CHAPTER FORTY-FIVE

Did a 1947 Chevy from Manitoba End Up in Eastern Ontario?

J ack Glover is a greeter at Walmart here in my home town of Leamington, Ontario, and reads my column in the *Wheatley Journal*. He is perfect as a greeter because he is always smiling and cheerful and always happy to help customers find what they are looking for.

I was in the store one day and asked Jack what he could tell me about his first car. It was a lime-green 1947 Chevrolet four-door sedan in running condition. He bought it in the early 1950s for $200 while living in southern Manitoba between Morden and Winkler.

His car was equipped with a vacuum-assisted three-speed gearshift on the steering column and the vacuum assist was designed to make gear changes almost effortless. This feature was installed on the car at the GM factory and no doubt worked properly when the car was new. By the time Jack got the car, shifting gears in the dead of a Manitoba winter was a real chore because the vacuum assist was no longer of any assistance.

That's me, the "Old Car Detective," in a wrecking yard in eastern Ontario alongside what might have been Jack Glover's first car.

He also remembers installing storm windows on the car. They were held in place with rubber suction cups and came from the local Canadian Tire store.

Under Jack's hood was the famous "Blue Flame" overhead valve 6-cylinder engine with 216 cubic inches cranking out 90 horsepower at 3300 rpm. It was not an oil burner and the previous owner probably took good care of it. Fuel economy was quite reasonable, and Jack's friends who rode with him often donated nickels and dimes every time he pulled in for gas.

The car ran fine until one day it popped a piston. Jack and his friends parked the car in a barn and took the engine all apart to fix the problem. They managed to get it put back together, but then it ran even worse than before. Finally, Jack took his car to a licensed mechanic to have it fixed properly.

Jack never took a photo of his car and never saw it again after he sold it over fifty years ago. Is there any chance it might still be around? My work as the Old Car Detective often takes me to old vintage auto wreckers in out-of-the-way places. I often photograph the derelict cars slowly rusting away and wonder who was behind the wheel when they were last on the road.

Around 1999, I visited Elliott's Auto Parts near Newtonville, Ontario. While roaming through the pitiful automotive remains, I had my picture taken alongside a rusting-away lime green 1947 Chevrolet sedan. I now ask myself, *Could this be Jack Glover's first car if the fellow who bought it from him later moved to eastern Ontario?* A few years after the picture was taken, the crushers came in and the car that might have been Jack's has gone to the big scrapyard in the sky.

CHAPTER FORTY-SIX

Hitchhiker Refused Second Ride in Oil-Burning 1947 Hudson

Ron Pickford grew up in the west end of Toronto in the 1950s. His cousin Richard owned a dull grey 1948 Chevrolet coach. It was a high-mileage car, but he got it cheap.

One day, while Richard was driving it, the left front motor mount disintegrated from rust and the engine then leaned to one side. The car was still driveable, but the gearshift linkage was now out of alignment and the vibration threatened to break the other motor mount.

Being short on cash, Ron and Richard took the scissor jack out of the trunk and wedged it between the frame and the engine, then jacked up the engine until it was upright. The old Chevy was now back on the road, but it still looked shabby. It was time to trade up to something better.

The boys found a black 1947 Hudson in the front row of a used-car lot on Lakeshore Boulevard and stopped to look it over. Under the hood was a huge flathead straight-8 engine and the car was a four-door sedan — ideal for dating at a drive-in movie.

The salesman could see the boys were hooked. He looked at the 1948 Chev and even started it up, but didn't look under the hood, where the jack was still propping up the engine. Ron and Richard paid

1947 Hudson Commodore four-door sedan in the sales brochure.

$75 plus the 1948 Chev and the Hudson was theirs. Just before driving away, Richard looked in the trunk and saw the Hudson had no jack. When the salesman wasn't looking, the boys retrieved the jack from under the hood of the 1948 Chev and tossed it into the trunk of the Hudson, then drove away!

They soon discovered the Hudson burned oil. It smoked so much that Ron and Richard went through a gallon of oil every time they drove from Toronto to Buffalo (ninety-two miles or 148 kilometres), and another gallon on the way home. The fumes were so bad inside the car that Richard wore a snorkel mask with an air tube sticking out through the driver's window.

One day, they picked up a soldier hitchhiking near Camp Borden. He sat in the back seat with his duffle bag. The fumes were so heavy that the boys could hardly see him. Then a heater hose burst open under the dash and filled the car with steam. After that they couldn't see the soldier at all.

They pulled off the highway and rolled to a stop. The soldier got out and began hitchhiking again while the boys tried to fix the leak. They looked under the hood and discovered the heater hose had extra slack. They cut off the broken piece, reattached the hose, and were back on the road in less than fifteen minutes.

The soldier by now was half a mile up the road and still hitch-hiking. They pulled over and offered him another ride and he said, "No, thanks."

CHAPTER FORTY-SEVEN

Another 1947 Mercury Convertible Nearly Forty Years Later

Mike Thorpe lives in North Vancouver, British Columbia, and is the proud owner of a very rare car, a 1947 Mercury 114 convertible. Based on the 1946 to 1948 Ford wheelbase, this model was built only in Canada. Only forty of these open cars were built by Ford of Canada in 1946 and only thirty-eight in 1947.

A few years ago, Mike Thorpe met Alyn Edwards, a car collector who writes for *Old Autos* newspaper. Mike describes what happened next:

> I mentioned to Alyn that if he ever heard of a 1947 Mercury convertible for sale to let me know because I owned a 1947 Mercury 118 convertible from 1954 to 1957 here in B.C. About two years later, he called to

This spectacular view of Mike Thorpe's 1947 Mercury 114 convertible makes you want to climb in and take it for a spin.

say a man named Dan Campbell near Sydney, Nova Scotia, was selling one for a widow whose husband had purchased it from Dan some eight years earlier. But it wasn't a 118. It was a 114.

Well, I wanted it, so Alyn contacted a friend to go and take a look at it. He said it was okay, so Alyn arranged for it to be delivered to my home in North Vancouver in August 1993. New to the old car hobby, I met Dick Parton, who encouraged me to join the Early Ford V8 Club the following year. That helped a lot in finding parts and made for a great social life with a good many friends.

By 1996, the lacquer finish on the car looked very tired. Brett Richards painted airplanes and offered to help me repaint the car. We began by removing the chrome and fenders and body filler and so it went, until many months later when the final coat went on. It is finished in gleaming burgundy, the colour of the car when I bought it. During the restoration, we discovered that the car had changed colour several times in the past. It had been red and white and dark blue, and probably changed colour as the car changed hands from owner to owner.

My wife and I went across Canada after I bought my 1947 Mercury 114 and went over to Cape Breton Island, where we stopped in to see Dan Campbell, the man who sold me my car. His home is an ex-motel and half the building is a long garage filled with many cars. He told me he had bought my Mercury twelve years before I bought it (that would be around 1981). He had gone to Toronto with his trailer to pick up some other cars, but they had been sold before he got there. As he was heading home, he spotted the Mercury convertible behind a garage in Toronto and towed it home.

Mike Thorpe owned his first 1947 Mercury convertible from 1954 to 1957. He bought it in September 1954 in North Vancouver from a logger, George Guelph, and only three of these cars were registered in British Columbia at that time. It was in excellent condition with its gleaming black original finish. The interior was tan leather, the top was black, and it was equipped with a Columbia two-speed rear axle. The mileage was in the mid-twenties as George was away logging all summer and didn't seem to drive it much in the winter.

George Guelph had purchased it in Victoria from a bank manager's wife, who got it brand new in 1947.

Mike sold his convertible in November 1957 as winter was coming on and he was working on the tugboats. He was married by then and his wife's grandmother was always saying that a convertible was not a family man's car. Mike and his wife traded the convertible in at Lawson Oats Motors for a 1951 Pontiac Chieftain hardtop. Thirty-six years later, Mike bought the Mercury convertible he owns today.

CHAPTER FORTY-EIGHT

1948 Chrysler Had Very Colourful Speedometer

Rick Herbert of Grimsby, Ontario, reads my column in the *Hamilton Spectator*. He has many stories to tell. Here is one of them:

> In the late 1950s, my father, Harry Herbert of Crystal Beach, Ontario, took ownership of a car owned by his father, William Herbert of Ridgeville, Ontario. It

Rick Herbert's father and sister Cathy are sitting on the rear bumper of their 1948 Chrysler in 1961. The high roofline, dictated by Chrysler president K.T. Keller, enabled a man to drive the car without removing his hat, which back then was usually a fedora.

was a black 1948 Chrysler four-door sedan, a massive car with "suicide doors" at the rear. The doors opened in opposite directions and closed at the centre post between the doors.

The original owner had installed seat covers front and rear to protect them over the years, and when they were taken off, the seats were just like they came from the factory. They were made of a dark blue velvet-like material and looked fit for king or queen.

The car had a semi-automatic transmission. You hardly ever had to shift gears, but when you were going fast enough in first gear, you would take your foot off the gas and the car would automatically shift into second. I believe this was the same system for shifting into third.

The speedometer was lit in such a way that the dial would change colour as you went faster, changing gradually from shades of green at low speeds through yellow and orange to red at high speeds. This was a neat feature and interesting to watch as the colours changed. It was marketed as the "Safety-Signal" speedometer and appeared for the first time on Chrysler-built cars in 1939.

Not far from Crystal Beach is the Point Abino Lighthouse. One section of the road leading to the lighthouse is very close to the shore, and not very high above the usual water line. On one excursion to see the lighthouse on a very windy day, we saw some waves lapping over this section of the road. By the time we returned from the lighthouse, the road was completely flooded. As we drove slowly through the water, it got as high as the bottom of the doors, and the waves were even higher, but we made it through.

The semi-automatic transmission in the Herbert family's Chrysler was known as Fluid Drive and the Chrysler Corporation took great precautions to make sure that motorists gave it proper care. A factory warning stated: "The fluid used in the coupling must be of the correct chemical analysis and viscosity. This fluid is obtainable ONLY through the Chrysler Parts Corporation, and no other should be used under any circumstances."

CHAPTER FORTY-NINE

1948 Studebaker: Great Style But Burned Oil

*J*im Love lives in Grimsby, Ontario, and reads this column in the Hamilton Spectator. Here is his story:

It was 1955. I was nineteen and had just graduated from teachers' college and was hired to teach at a one-room country school at Brodhagen, Ontario, fifteen miles from our farm and about thirty-five miles northeast of Exeter. I had to buy a car.

I looked around on my own and found this lovely sleek and shiny black 1948 Studebaker Commander four-door sedan with wire wheels and a radio. It had lots of chrome, the steering wheel looked fancy, and the dashboard was better than any I had ever seen. This car's style was ahead of its time! The price was $500. I thought I could manage it so I bought it.

Well, the car had been over the roads and had more miles on it than I knew. I did a motor job on it, then decided to drive up to Copper

1948 Studebaker Commander four-door sedan in the sales brochure. Note the rear-hinged, front-opening rear doors, often referred to as "suicide doors" because of the danger of passengers falling out if the door flew open at high speed.

Cliff, Ontario, (just past Sudbury) to visit my sister, who was teaching there. It was a long drive in those days, about three hundred miles. I probably shouldn't have driven the car so hard just after a motor job because when I got to Copper Cliff, I was nearly out of oil.

Ever after that, the car used oil. However, it still ran well and ticked along like a sewing machine. A couple of years later, I was still driving it, but in the hot summer weather I was pouring axle grease in for oil. The oil gauge would spring right over to top pressure when you started the car, then after a lot of driving would fall lower and lower.

In spite of all this, it was a pleasure to drive. The car had bench seats, which were very comfortable and it steered and held the road nicely. This Studebaker had one feature which I have never found on another car. It was a hill holder. When you pressed down on the clutch when stopped on a hill, a brake came on and the car would not roll backwards.

Around 1958, the next car I got was a 1952 Ford V-8 sedan. Boy, did that car have power! But that's another story ...

Jim Love's 1948 Studebaker may have been built in Hamilton. The Studebaker Corporation of South Bend, Indiana, opened a plant in Hamilton in August 1948 and manufactured cars at that facility until 1966, when the last Studebaker rolled off the assembly line and into history, a casualty of competition from the Big Three.

CHAPTER FIFTY

1949 Ford: He Rode on a Donkey Before He Rode in a Car

Camille Peters was born in 1946 and spent his first few years in his family's native land of Lebanon. When he was around five, he remembers a neighbour on their street who owned a donkey, and all the young children were eager to go for a ride.

One day, the donkey was parked beside a big rock and this enabled some children to climb on. Three of them sat one behind the other and told Camille (the smallest and youngest) to step down off the rock and ride at the back end of the donkey.

Apparently the extra weight was too much for the donkey and he kicked his hind legs high in the air. Camille went flying off and crash-landed on the ground with cuts and scrapes and bruises. He was bleeding from his forehead and was rushed to a nearby hospital where he was bandaged up and sent home. Years later, all four children on that donkey are now living in Canada and Camille makes his home in Leamington, the Tomato Capital of Canada.

Newspaper ad for the new 1949 Ford.

Some of our readers might think it odd that this column would include the story of a boy who fell off a donkey. Actually, there is a close connection between cars and horses, and by extension donkeys, too. We speak of a car having headlights and tail lights, and yet where is the head and where is the tail? These terms have come down to us from the days of horses and buggies.

And speaking of buggies, if you rode in one pulled by a horse (or donkey), you would notice a board sticking up at the front of the buggy. That board was there to protect you from the mud flying up from the hooves of the galloping animal, and the mud got dashed against the board instead of all over you. When people began building automobiles, they needed a board in front of the driver and passenger to hold the instruments. To this very day, we still refer to that instrument panel as a dashboard. And we still measure the power output of an engine in horsepower.

When Camille was a teenager living in Leamington, he was eager to drive a car and take his girlfriend to the local drive-in movie theatre. His dad was not too eager to loan him the family car — a 1949 Ford. But after his dad fell asleep and was snoring, Camille would reach under his dad's pillow where he had hidden the car keys and go for a ride. As he got older, he bought a car of his own, but that's another story …

CHAPTER FIFTY-ONE

1949 "Heinz 57" International Truck

I'm writing these words in Leamington, Ontario, the Tomato Capital of Canada, home of the H.J. Heinz Co. of Canada Ltd., and home of Dennis Jackson, a retired Heinz employee and collector of Heinz memorabilia for the past forty years.

Dennis Jackson with his 1949 International truck celebrating one hundred years of Heinz Canada in Leamington, Ontario.

Long-time tomato farmer Herm Dick poses with pride alongside Dennis Jackson's "Heinz 57" pickup truck. Herm and his wife Elizabeth have travelled all over the world, and wherever they go, Herm hands out Heinz pickle pins to everyone they meet. Herm Dick also has been featured in the television program The Great Canadian Food Show. *On the back of this photo, his friend Dennis Jackson wrote, "My career has ended, but Herm's has just begun."*

Dennis Jackson has now accumulated over ten thousand items that chronicle the history of the H.J. Heinz Company, which began in Pittsburgh, Pennsylvania, in 1869, and came to Leamington in 1909. Jackson's collection includes pickle pins, old-time ketchup bottles, soup labels, magazine ads, awards for faithful service, employee uniforms, promotional items, hundreds of rare old photos, toy trucks, newspaper clippings, sales brochures, company memos, letters, and all the personal memorabilia of my father, Frank T. Sherk, the first Canadian-born president of the H.J. Heinz Co. of Canada Ltd., donated to the collection by the Sherk family in 1994.

The largest item by far in Dennis's collection is his 1949 International KB-1 pickup truck. It faithfully reproduces the traditional colour scheme of Heinz trucks — all white with a flat black hood and correct Heinz lettering on the doors.

Jackson's truck spent many years stored in a barn in western Canada. The original colour was dark blue. It arrived in Leamington in the mid-1990s when purchased by the late Kurt Gossen, owner of the local Land Mercury dealership. Kurt painted the truck in traditional Heinz colours, and then it sat in the back of his shop for the next three years. Kurt's untimely death in 1997 set off a chain of events that led to Dennis purchasing the truck later that year.

The mechanical restoration was performed by Vince Finaldi and his brother Henry of Nationwide Canning in Cottam, Ontario. Further work was performed by H. & J. Auto Clinic in Leamington, and the truck was ready for the road by August 1998.

On January 4, 2000, Dennis Jackson turned fifty-seven, the magic number here in Leamington with Heinz "57 varieties." To help celebrate his birthday, a group of friends got together and ordered special license plates for Dennis's truck: HEINZ 57. His truck has been a familiar sight around town for the past ten years, and 2009 marked a special milestone with the celebration of Heinz of Canada's 100th anniversary in Leamington. Dennis drove his truck in the Tomato Festival parade through town on Saturday, August 15, 2009, while blowing all five of his horns and waving to all the well-wishers lining the parade route through Leamington.

CHAPTER FIFTY-TWO

1949 Monarch Off the Road Since 1958

Duringthe 1990s, I frequently visited Elliott Auto Parts on Hwy. 2, just east of Newtonville, Ontario. At that time, it was one of the largest vintage wrecking yards in Canada. Over the past decade, most of the cars have gone to the crusher, but one car that escaped that fate is the 1949 Monarch four-door sedan pictured here (the Monarch first appeared in 1946 as a companion car to the Mercury and was built only in Canada).

I first saw this car around 1997 near the swamp at the back of the yard while accompanied by my good friend Vern Kipp, a past president of the Southern Ontario Region of the Early Ford V-8 Club of America. Our attention was immediately drawn to the grille consisting of three original 1949 Monarch horizontal grille bars with the original vertical grille bars removed to give the car a customized look.

Vern Kipp stands next to this 1949 Monarch with a customized grille and "Buick" portholes when I snapped this picture around 1997.

We also took note of the three portholes on the front fenders, similar to those on a 1949 Buick and available from Canadian Tire as aftermarket items. Clearly, this car was owned by a young person when it was last on the road. He (or she!) would now be in his or her seventies, and if they see this story, they might tell us more about this car.

When we examined the rear of the car, we discovered the trunk lid and tail lights were gone, presumably to help restore another 1949 Monarch. But the 1958 licence plate (black on white) from when this car was last on the road was still attached to the rear bumper.

In 2002, Vern returned to Elliott's Auto Parts and purchased the pitiful remains of this once-proud 1949 Monarch. He had the car transported to the farm of his good friend Noel Hamer near Odessa in eastern Ontario, where it resides to this day as a parts car to assist in the restoration of other Monarchs and Mercurys. The dashboard has gone to a fellow in Collingwood and the rear splash pan has gone to another restoration project in St. Catharines.

CHAPTER FIFTY-THREE

Dan Stephens's Dream Car: His 1949 Monarch Sport Sedan

Dan Stephens of Port Credit, Ontario, reads my "Old Car Detective" column in the *Mississauga News*. He is the proud owner of a 1949 Monarch Sport sedan.

Ford of Canada introduced the Monarch in 1946, based on the Mercury of that year, but with unique grille and trim and built only in Canada. On May 1, 1948, a totally new Monarch and Mercury were unveiled for 1949. Low and wide with classic styling, these cars are highly collectible today.

Dan Stephens purchased his Monarch in 2007 from the RM classic car auction in amazing original condition: "The car is a four-door with suicide doors and is painted in the original medium blue metallic," says Dan. "It has the original interior, all working gauges, Monarch

Daniel Stephens's beautiful and all-original 1949 Monarch Sport sedan.

nameplates, original working radio, and the original flathead V-8. Although not of museum quality, I purchased it as a driver to enjoy cruising around Port Credit with my wife and three sons."

Dan's Monarch also has original matching 1949 Ontario licence plates and Coker classic whitewall tires on factory wheel rims finished in red with original hubcaps.

Ever since Dan was a teenager, he has always had an interest in the Mercury and Monarch cars from 1949 to 1951:

> I love their flowing lines, high roof line, and massive chrome bumpers. I was particularly interested in this Monarch because it has never been customized. The previous owner told me the car had resided in a barn for several decades and he had performed some minor body work on the rear fenders.
>
> Research indicates that only 11,317 Monarchs were built for the 1949 model year, which means it is a fairly rare car.
>
> Now here's an interesting story. My wife said to go and get the classic car I always wanted for my 40th birthday. I was originally after a Mustang, but I started bidding on the Monarch because as soon as I saw it, I knew that's the car I wanted. A few months after I bought the car, I noticed that I had circled and written "What a beautiful car!" in a previous auction catalogue only to later end up owning that very same car.
>
> With three young boys, it is not always easy to get to car shows, but I plan to attend some next summer as time allows. I still go to auctions and look for interesting cars — and I am always on the lookout for a 1965 to 1968 Mustang. I enjoy all classic cars whether they be Fords, Chevys, cruisers, or muscle cars, but my 1949 Monarch will always be my dream car.

CHAPTER FIFTY-FOUR

Driving Across Europe in a "1949" Volkswagen

*J*erry Dick *grew up in the southwestern Ontario town of Ruthven and now lives in Mississauga, where he reads my column in the* Mississauga News. *After graduating from Engineering at the University of Western Ontario in the spring of 1970, he headed off to Europe for work, adventure, and a set of wheels.*

I met her on a cold, drizzling morning in a small southern Bavarian town. She stood alone, small, unmistakably used and abused, but to me she was the most beautiful thing I had ever seen. Forty dollars and she was mine — a 1949 Volkswagen. Footsore and weary, I gratefully eased my aching frame behind the small, white, cracked steering wheel. Ahead of us lay many thousands of miles of unknown and occasionally hostile European countryside throughout which she became my trusted and utterly reliable companion.

The early hours of our trip were spent in reaching the French border, where we were subjected to an auto search. That's when I

Jerry Dick enjoyed the sun roof on his Volkswagen in Europe in 1970. Note air vent on side of body ahead of door.

learned two things about travelling in Europe. Always keep the glove compartment full of official-looking papers and never drop the guise of a super-helpless tourist. After France was Switzerland, where I soon realized there was more than one Canadian in Europe. I was later to meet Nova Scotians in Germany, British Columbians in Austria, and Ontarians in Holland.

After crossing the Swiss-Austrian border, we were forced to climb higher and higher into the Alps. We passed the treeline, the grass line, and entered the snow line. The determined little VW, in first gear, chugged bravely onward into the sky. We reached the crest of the Arlberg Pass and then the fun really began on the downward descent. With ancient brakes and an arthritic transmission, we wouldn't have got there much sooner had we fallen off the mountain.

Leaving Austria, my VW and I made a mad dash across Germany to see as much of Europe as possible before the flight home. We passed Munich, where construction crews had mangled every street in frenzied preparation for the 1972 Olympics. Even the detours had detours. Crossing into Denmark, I parked on the beach and had my first swim in salt water. Returning fifteen minutes later, I saw a crowd standing knee-deep in water while admiring my car (the tide had come in). Jumping inside, I started her and spluttered across the fifty feet of sea water to firm sand.

I visited two more countries before racing for the rendezvous with the KLM charter flight from Frankfurt. My car and I travelled seven thousand kilometres together and it was with great sadness that I parted with my little Teutonic friend.

Jerry Dick was told his VW was a '49. Matt Jenner of North Ridge, Ontario, writes: "Jerry's VW is a 1951 or 1952 deluxe model. I can tell by the 'crotch coolers' in the front quarter panel of the car. The 1951 and 1952 models were the only ones that had these strange vents."

CHAPTER FIFTY-FIVE

The Day I Drove a 1950 Meteor Convertible

In May 1958, and long before I became known as the Old Car Detective, I turned sixteen, got my driver's licence, and began shopping around for a used car in Leamington. The car that caught my eye was a gleaming black 1950 Meteor convertible with whitewall tires and fender skirts. The top was down and it was parked in the front row of Jackson's used car lot on Talbot St. East, now the parking lot for the Half Century Club.

I leaned in and checked the odometer: eighty-five thousand miles. A salesman suddenly appeared and told me I could drive this car home for "only $650." I told him I didn't have that much money, but if I could talk my older brother into buying the car with me, we could swing a deal. John was working that summer in the parts department of Ray Young's Pontiac-Buick dealership at 11 Mill Street East.

Then the salesman said: "The keys are in the car. Drive it uptown and show it to your brother." I could hardly believe my ears. I slid behind the wheel and turned the key. Then I pressed the starter button.

1950 Meteor convertible in the sales brochure. When I test-drove a car like this, I imagined I would have at least two girlfriends, just like the lucky fellow in this picture.

The flathead V8 roared to life with a rumbling noise under the floor. This car had Hollywood mufflers!

I pulled the gearshift down into first, then gave it some gas as I let out the clutch. The car began moving off the lot. I headed west along the main street with the sun shining down and the wind in my hair. I was in heaven!

I stopped for a red light in front of Jack Hartford's Texaco station at Talbot East and Victoria, hoping people would see me behind the wheel. Then the light turned green and I headed south along Victoria Street, lined on both sides with big shade trees. I looked above the windshield and could see the trees passing right above my head. What a thrill! This was the first time I drove a convertible, and the first time I even had a ride in one.

I parked in front of the dealership where my brother worked and showed him the Meteor. Then he showed me another car. Earlier that morning, Ray Young had taken in a low mileage 1940 Buick Super coupe in showroom condition. Someone else bought the Meteor and we bought the 1940 Buick for $500. It stayed in our family for thirty years.

CHAPTER FIFTY-SIX

Perfect Car for Young Family: A New 1950 Dodge Coupe

Elsie Buie of Midhurst, Ontario, passed away in March 2006 at ninety-one. A few months later, her daughter, Catherine Walsh-Riediger (formerly of Stroud and past president of the Innisfil Chamber of Commerce), found papers that told the story of a 1950 Dodge D36 coupe purchased new by her late father, Bill McGinnis, on December 29, 1950, from Dangerfield Motors, a Dodge-DeSoto dealership located then at 65 Collier Street in downtown Barrie.

Catherine and her mother and dad were living at that time in a house at 75 McDonald Street near the downtown area. The dealership would have been a short walk from the McGinnis house. The base price of the car was $1994.50. Extras included a heater, two gallons of anti-freeze, licence, finance charges, and other miscellaneous items bringing the total to $2180.70.

Catherine's dad paid for the car with a $400 down payment, a trade-in worth $696.20 (his 1941 Chevrolet coach), twelve monthly payments of $58, and another $400 upon delivery of the new Dodge. (Just after this, Dangerfield Motors became a GM dealership and relocated a few

This Dodge Custom coupe is similar to the Dodge D36 coupe purchased by Bill McGinnis from Dangerfield Motors in Barrie, Ontario, on Friday, December 29, 1950.

years later to Bradford Street). A two-door coupe was a good choice for Bill and Elsie McGinnis because their daughter Catherine was not yet six years old when the Dodge was purchased. She could safely romp around in the big back seat while Mom and Dad sat up front.

Bill McGinnis was an engineer with Canadian National. Around 1952, he was transferred from Barrie to Nakina in northern Ontario, where the family lived for the next two years. Nakina was so far north that it could only be reached at that time by air or rail. All four members of the family (Dad, Mother, Catherine, and a beagle named Sport) piled into the 1950 Dodge and headed north. The Dodge had to be stored in a garage at Longlac and the family travelled the remaining distance by train.

Bill McGinnis knew the posting to Nakina was not permanent, and the family travelled back and forth between there and Barrie several times in their 1950 Dodge. On those trips, Catherine's dad always brought along his tackle and would often pull off the highway to go trout fishing. Mom and the dog waited in the car while Catherine joined her dad. One day, it was so hot, the dog jumped out of the car and went for a swim in the trout stream.

Under the hood of every 1950 Dodge was a very reliable flathead 6-cylinder engine with 230 cubic inches cranking out 105 horsepower. The McGinnis Dodge served the family well for several years until it was traded in for a 1955 Chevrolet.

CHAPTER FIFTY-SEVEN

He Dated His Future Bride in His 1951 Chevy Fleetline Fastback

*J*ean-Claude Marcoux is a retired chiropractor living in Mont St.-Hilaire, Quebec, with his wife of fifty-four years, Lucille. They both remember his first car because they dated in it before they got married! Here is the story that takes us back to Montreal in 1956.

Jean-Claude Marcoux was nineteen when he bought his 1951 Chevy Fleetline fastback in the winter of 1955–56 and had to wash it frequently to remove the snow that Montreal winters are famous for. He made arrangements with the owner of this Supertest gas station on Pie IX Boulevard in Montreal's east end to wash his car himself during off hours in the warm comfort of one of the service bays. Little did he realize when he posed for this photo that it would adorn the front cover of this book over fifty years later! During those fifty-plus years, Jean-Claude has owned an amazing number of interesting cars, including a 1953 Kaiser Manhattan, a 1954 Nash Ambassador Country Club hardtop, a 1961 Thunderbird convertible, and a 1967 Olds Toronado.

I need a car of my own! I make an honest sixty bucks a week and I still live with my parents, but I can't afford an expensive car. My boss has a brother who sells Chrysler products in Verdun. There I see a beat-up-looking 1951 Chevy Fleetline Deluxe four-door fastback with automatic transmission. I find her dashing and full of potential.

For the outrageous price of $600, the dealer will fix everything, put in a new battery, and give it a new paint job and thorough cleaning inside. Since they'll redo the outside, I demand some changes to give my first chariot a "modern look." They took chrome pieces off the hood and trunk so I'll have that very desirable shaved look. And please, since I can't afford a V-8, install a dummy dual exhaust on the back so it looks like I have one. "Okay, sir," came the reply. I'm trembling with fear and delicious anticipation as I sign the necessary papers.

The folks at the dealer really did a great job. It was like taking delivery of a brand-new automobile! It rode as good as it looked, and I thought no other car on the road was as beautiful as mine. Free at last! Free to go where and when I feel … oh sweet liberty! How I do love thee! The summer of 1956 was heaven on earth for me. But more bliss would come my way before that year was over …

On Saturday, September 29, I get a phone call from a college buddy's girlfriend. She has a friend she wants to introduce to me. At first I'm not interested … but when she describes a beautiful blonde with fantastic qualities, I say, "Okay, give me her address. I'll change and pick her up and we'll meet you at the Faison Bleu (a very popular Montreal dance hall in those days)."

When I get in front of her house, I park carefully, take another satisfied look at my blue fastback, and ring the bell. There she stands at the top of the stairway, the most beautiful female I've ever contemplated, all smiling and so gorgeous in that bright dress over a large crinoline. "Hi, I'm Jean-Claude!"

"Hi, I'm Lucille."

Walking toward my Chevy, she takes an interested look at it and says with enthusiasm, "Wow! You've got a beautiful car!" Music to my ears, I tell you. I was hooked right then and there. It was indeed a fateful encounter. Little did we both know on that beautiful September evening that we'd be married one year and eight days later, that we'd eventually have four beautiful children and that those kids would, in time, give us ten grandchildren.... We celebrated our fiftieth wedding anniversary in 2007.

CHAPTER FIFTY-EIGHT

Tooling Around Halifax in an Old 1951 Chrysler Windsor Deluxe

*T*erry Halverson enjoys reading my column in the Moncton Times & Transcript. *He has fond memories of his first car:*

I bought it in 1968 when I was seventeen and working as a gas station jockey part-time, pumping gas and taking an apprentice mechanics course on weekends at Doug Marriot's Esso in Halifax.

The car was a 1951 Chrysler Windsor Deluxe. A flathead six with tons of chrome, four doors, AM radio, and padded upholstery you sank six inches deep into. Wow! I was in heaven. An awesome machine, even though it was well used and probably looked shabby to everyone else, it was a gem to me. Vacuum wipers and one of the first automatic transmissions that ran by having two big fans inside the tranny about a quarter inch apart that drove the fluid to each other.

1951 Chrysler Windsor sedan in the sales brochure: "You can and will be proud of your new 1951 Chrysler ... a car that will reflect your discriminating taste ... a car that will be in keeping with your home and your other fine possessions ... and, most of all, a car that your friends and associates will admire and respect. Pictured here is the graceful styling of the new rear window that gives you observation-car vision ..."

I paid $75 for this baby and took possession one night in the pouring rain. Driving it was like floating on air. Although I couldn't afford the full insurance because I was still in school, I got the basic, and we tooled around Halifax that summer of love.

I forget what the weight of that puppy was, but it whizzed along and floated like a '71 Cadillac I owned later on. That one was over 4600 pounds.

When I went back to school that winter, I had to store the car outside at the garage, and as a result it was badly vandalized. All the upholstery was shredded and cut into ribbons. The windshield, dash, radio, and one side window were smashed. Someone had partied in it and there were broken beer bottles and wine spilled all over the interior.

I almost cried. Not having the money to fix it properly, I figured I had to let it go. I took off the widetrack Esso tires I had installed, put on the old ones I had saved from when I bought it, and advertised it for junk.

To my amazement, a gentleman called me a week later and said he had one just like it and he needed a body (mine was in excellent shape). I wanted to buy his for the interior and the glass and he wanted mine for the body. He wouldn't sell his. He offered me $150, twice what I had paid for it, so I let it go.

It was a sad day when he pulled it up on the tow sled and drove off. But, being a teenager, I smiled and went to look at a 1964 Ford Galaxie I had been eyeing. Now, those cars back then were cars, not beer-can-thin little boxes. They had style.

Anyway, love your articles and keep up the great storytelling.

CHAPTER FIFTY-NINE

The Amazing Story of a Purple 1951 Monarch Convertible

K ent Weale grew up in Port Credit, Ontario, where he still lives. His first car was a weather-beaten 1940 Ford coupe, which he brought home in 1960 when he was sixteen. His father told him to park it in the garage and shut the door so the neighbours wouldn't have to look at it.

Kent sold the '40 in 1962 after putting a Buick engine in it. Then he heard about a customized 1951 Monarch convertible for sale in Oakville. The car had no engine or transmission, but would be "a steal at $85." As Kent recalls: "My ride at the time was a '56 Chevy 6-cylinder

Here is Kent's Monarch soon after bringing it home in the spring of 1963.

stick with dual straight pipes and traction bars. Nice little car, but here was a chance for a ragtop and already customized. Every teenage guy's dream car!"

Unable to resist, Kent bought the car, but could not bring it home. "My mother would have gone nuts if she knew that I had bought another car, so I made arrangements to hide it behind Burton's Supertest gas station on Hwy. 10 in Port Credit. A few weeks later, a friend and I towed it to Streetsville, where it spent the winter."

Meanwhile, Kent had to get an engine. The car was set up for a Y-block Ford V-8, so he decided to use a similar engine. Peter Clancy, a friend of Kent, lined up a modified 1957 312 from a local hot rodder, Donny Cloake, out of his hot 1956 Ford. Don didn't have a place to lift the engine out, so when it was disconnected, Kent and some friends pushed the car to a vacant lot with a suitable tree. Kent remembers that night well:

> With the engine up in the air, we shoved the Ford back-
> wards just out of the way, and backed my Chevy under
> it with the trunk lid removed. We lowered the engine
> down into the trunk. Then we tied the cars together

The 1957 Y-block V-8 has just been dropped into the Monarch after denting the top of the left front fender.

> using the same chain from the tree branch. Peter and
> another friend sat on each rear fender and kept the
> engine from falling over. Don steered the Ford while

we pulled it back to his house. We then proceeded down Brown's Line, along the Lakeshore, and up Dixie Road with Peter and friend still perched on the rear fenders. There were no police in sight that night and we dropped the engine off at a rented garage.

The next spring, a friend let Kent keep the car at his place for a couple of weeks while his parents were away. Now the Monarch was closer to home but his mother still didn't know about it. Kent picked a time when she would be out all evening, towed the car home through the snow, and, using a large borrowed tripod, dropped the Y-block engine into the Monarch. In his haste, the engine dented the left front fender, and that dent would help to identify the car over thirty years later.

Kent's mother arrived home just after the car was returned to the friend's house. Then she went on vacation and the Monarch came home. When Mom got home and calmed down, the Monarch stayed.

Kent sold it in 1966 in order to buy a hot rodded 1934 Ford coupe, his next project.

Nearly thirty years after Kent Weale sold his 1951 Monarch, he and I decided to search for the man who painted it purple and to see if the car was still around. Kent had purchased it from Gary McKinney in Oakville, who only had it a month when his father told him to get rid of it. We contacted Gary and he told us he had bought it from a man in Milton, but because Gary was colour-blind, he didn't even know the car was purple.

In early March 1995, Kent got a phone call from Jim Newell, who remembered the car from the Milton area, and nearly bought it himself in 1962, but changed his mind while road-testing it. The Ford Y-block V-8 under the hood (not the same engine Kent later used) was in pretty sad shape, and when Jim tried to drag race a flat-top 1952 Ford from a red light, the flat-top beat the Monarch. Jim remembered that the man selling the Monarch was Brian MacDuffee. He was later killed in a snowmobile accident.

Then we talked to Bern Fritshaw on March 26, 1995, at the Rodmasters Swap Meet in Ancaster, Ontario. Thanks to Bern, we were able to find the man who owned the car when it turned purple. On Sunday, April 9, 1995, Kent and I turned into Art Wiley's driveway in the village of Jordan, south of St. Catharines in the Niagara Peninsula. Art had owned Kent's 1951 Monarch ragtop from around 1958 to 1962, and had several photos of the car, including a colour photo showing the purple finish.

Art bought the Monarch at nearby Willard Auto Wreckers around 1958. The engine was not in good shape, but who cares? It was a convertible and it ran well enough for Art to drive it home. About a week later, the Monarch engine gave up completely and Art replaced it with a 312-cubic-inch 1957 Ford Y-block. He was now on the road again.

The Monarch was maroon when Art bought it, and the original colour had been Vasser Yellow. It needed body work and Art took it to Don Carter's garage in nearby Camden around 1960. Thirty-two bars of lead went into the car and finally it was ready for paint. Art wanted a classic fifties colour and that colour would have to be purple.

Don opened a can of light purple used as a stock colour on 1957 Cadillacs. Art looked at it and said it was too light. Don added a little darkener. Art said: "More ... more ... stop!" And that's how the Monarch got its shade of purple (also called mauve).

Art Wylie poses with pride alongside his 1951 Monarch convertible freshly repainted in mauve purple in 1960. Side trim and door handles have not yet been installed. He later sold it to Brian MacDuffee, who sold it to Gary McKinney, who sold it to Kent Weale.

Kent and I visited Don Carter's garage with Art, where the 1951 Monarch had turned purple thirty-five years earlier. When we arrived, Don was in the middle of getting a late-model pickup truck ready for a paint job. When we showed him Art Wylie's colour photo of the Monarch, his eyes lit up and he told us the pickup truck was parked on the exact spot on the floor of his garage where the Monarch received its body work and paint half a lifetime ago!

In 1962, Art Wylie sold the car to Brian MacDuffee in Milton, who sold it to Gary McKiney in Oakville, who sold it to Kent in Port Credit. Now the big question: was the Monarch still around and could we find it?

As mentioned earlier, Kent Weale sold his 1951 Monarch convertible in 1966 to work on his next project, a hot-rodded 1934 Ford coupe. In the spring, the Monarch, with its new owner, left the "Highwinders" car club barn in Streetsville with another Y-block just sitting in it. Kent happily went to work getting the 1934 ready for the road.

About a year later, the Monarch came back to haunt him once more. Kent got a letter from the police saying his 1951 Monarch had been impounded and would be sold for towing and storage costs if he didn't pay the same within five days. As it turned out, his "friend" hadn't transferred the ownership, nor had the person to whom he had sold the car. Kent called the police to explain the situation. They said he was welcome to come and see the car if he wanted to.

"My curiosity took me to an impound yard just off Kipling Avenue," recalls Kent. "There, a very sad and beat-up purple car sat up to its rockers in mud. The car looked awful: glass and tail lights smashed, chrome bent and broken, rusted and dented everywhere. I wasn't interested in getting it back and was sure it was headed for the crusher. Later I received a bunch of parking tickets that my 'friend' refused to pay. After paying them, I was sure the purple '51 Monarch was out of my life for good. It is amazing how wrong a person can be!"

Some thirty years later, Kent got a phone call from fellow old car enthusiast Bruce Beedie, who read in *Old Autos* about our search for his Monarch and said he owned a 1951 Monarch convertible in the 1980s. Kent and he got together and compared photos and details. Both cars had been nosed and decked with lead, drilled for spotlights, and equipped with lowering blocks. When Bruce found the car, it was flat black, but under that was a light mauve (light purple) colour. And under the mauve were traces of the car's original yellow paint. There were also traces of a white convertible top.

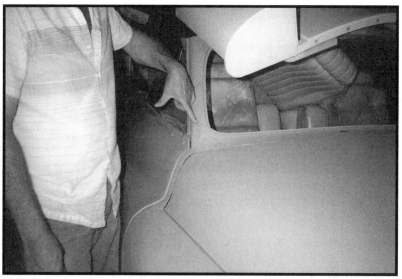

Kent Weale and I visited Casey Van Hamburg near Peterborough to see the 1951 Monarch convertible he had purchased from a man in London, Ontario. Kent is pointing to the spot on the windshield post where a hole had been drilled thirty years earlier for a spotlight. You can see where the hole has been filled in. He also found traces of the dent on the left front fender where he dropped the engine over thirty years earlier. This was the same car Kent had owned from 1962 to 1966.

Kent studied Bruce's photos with a magnifying glass. When he examined the left front fender, his eyes widened. "There was an angled dent on the top of the fender about twelve inches behind the headlight," recalls Kent. "I had inflicted that dent on a snowy night over thirty years ago when I literally dropped the engine onto the fender and then into the car. This was indeed the very same car."

Bruce Beedie and his wife had been living near London, Ontario, when he found the car at Chip's Scrap Metal Salvage Yard on Hwy. 3

near Courtland. It was in rough shape, but Bruce agreed to buy the car for $100. Then he changed his mind and passed the deal onto his friend Jim McCaughrin, who hauled it home. Mr. Chip told Bruce the car had come from the Muncie Reservation near Tillsonburg, where it had sat as a derelict for many years. Jim cleaned up the car, then sold it to Bruce, who later sold it to Dave Burridge, a London motorcycle dealer. Then the car was sold again, this time to Casey Van Hamburg in the Peterborough area. Kent and I visited Casey and finally found the Monarch we were looking for.

This is the car Kent Weale drives today, a 1933 Packard convertible. We were photographed arriving at a car show in Waterdown, Ontario. From right to left: Kent Weale (the man behind the wheel), Jim Dyson, Peter Minns, and me, Bill Sherk, a.k.a. the "Old Car Detective.

CHAPTER SIXTY

His 1952 Meteor Was the Coolest Car in Town

Ben Koop was born in 1935 and enjoys reading my column in the *Leamington Post*. After turning eighteen in 1953, he was ready to buy his first car and he knew exactly what he wanted — a Ford — because it would give him a V-8 engine along with great styling.

He visited all the used car lots around Tecumseh and Walker Road in nearby Windsor, and here on Noble Duff's used car lot, Ben found what he was looking for: a gleaming black 1952 Meteor Customline two-door sedan (the Canadian version of the Ford). The Customline

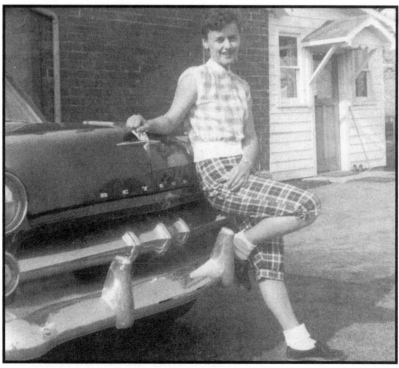

Ben Koop's future wife Margaret with his 1952 Meteor Customline. Note the missing front licence plate, removed by Ben three years earlier to give the front end a smoother look.

had a Mercury dashboard and a 255-cubic-inch Mercury flathead V-8 engine with 120 horsepower, along with a three-speed column-shift manual transmission ("three on the tree"), just what Ben was looking for. It had no radio, and that convinced Ben that the previous owner did not have a lead foot.

Noble Duff was well known for his large Mercury-Lincoln-Meteor dealership in downtown Windsor, and that's where Ben went to pay for his car: $1550 in cash in October 1953.

As soon as he drove it off the lot, Ben began to transform his Meteor into the coolest car in town. He started by removing the front licence plate to give the front of his car a smoother look. The front plate was still missing three years later when Ben's future wife, Margaret Toews, posed for a picture with the car.

Ben drove across the river to Detroit and purchased a Mercury radio, which had square push buttons (the less expensive Ford radio had round ones). After another trip to Detroit, you could hear him coming with dual exhausts and Thrush mufflers.

The H.J. Heinz Company in Leamington donated three-inch stainless steel pipes, which Ben used as tailpipe extensions that stuck out four inches beyond the rear bumper to protect the chrome from discolouration. These extensions were welded to the frame and Ben could stand on them without bending them.

Two local mechanics installed a dual ignition under the hood, and Ben removed the large four-blade fan from the front of the engine. This gave him more horsepower and better fuel economy, and whenever he began to overheat, he headed out of town for a run on the highway to cool the engine down.

Ben's car came from the Windsor factory with 6.70 x 15 tires. He replaced these with 7.10 x 15 tires from Baesinger General Tire at Woodward and Ten Mile Road in Detroit. This gave his car a higher top speed and he was clocked at a track doing 112 mph.

Baesinger was selling new "puncture-proof" tires and many owners of late model cars traded in their factory-installed tires. The trade-ins were sold as used tires, and some still had the green soap on the whitewalls because they had been someone's spare. Ben picked out five "used tires" off the rack and got five new tires at used-car prices.

He chose Firestones because they had a slightly narrower whitewall and they were whiter than the competition. Also, when stepping on the gas, Firestones made a better-sounding squeal than other brands.

Lowering the car in the rear end gave Ben's Meteor the "speedboat" look so popular back then. He bought two-inch lowering blocks and extra-long U-bolts in Detroit and also installed a 115-pound steel bar off a Caterpillar D8 bulldozer. This was placed at the extreme rear end of the trunk for maximum benefit. It also raised the front end slightly and made steering easier. Ben still has that steel bar.

In 1957, Ben married his sweetheart, Margaret Toews, and they drove the 1952 Meteor on their honeymoon to Florida. In Jacksonville, Ben walked into a bank to convert his Canadian money into American funds. The bank refused to do it!

Meanwhile, Marg was sitting in their 1952 Meteor parked outside. A well-dressed man with a diamond pin in his tie approached the car and asked Marg what it was. He knew it looked like a Ford, but wasn't a Ford. Just as she was explaining that the Meteor is the Canadian version of the Ford, Ben came out of the bank and told Marg the bad news about the bank refusing their money. And that's when the man looking at their car told them he knew the people in the bank and took Ben inside, where they cheerfully exchanged their money.

It pays to drive a Meteor to Florida!

Ben Koop owned his 1952 Meteor for seven years before trading it off for a Ford one-ton stake truck for his greenhouse business. He was allowed $900 for his Meteor and never saw it again.

CHAPTER SIXTY-ONE

Another 1952 Meteor Story with Newlyweds

*T*he story of Ben Koop's 1952 Meteor on the previous page was first published in my "Old Car Detective" column in Old Autos *newspaper on Monday, June 16, 2008. That paper goes all across Canada and is read by an estimated forty thousand readers every two weeks. Ben's story prompted Al Lawson to send in the following letter to Murray McEwan, the editor of* Old Autos.

Hi Murray: Well, here I am reporting from Lotus Land out here in Langley, B.C., and I have just read the article by the "Old Car Detective" Bill Sherk in the June 16th issue about Ben Koop's 1952 Meteor Customline two-door sedan. WOW! What a story and how it brought back memories for myself and my wife.

I too had a 1952 Meteor of the same vintage and I too have a picture of my future wife in her "pedal pushers" leaning on the car just like Ben's wife Margaret in the article. My wife and I were married on August 25, 1956, and the picture of Irene was taken on our honeymoon at the Grand Coulee Dam in Washington State.

This 1952 Meteor Mainline in the sales brochure is identical to the car owned by Al Lawson in British Columbia. The Mainline does not have the same side trim as the Customline and has a Ford engine and Ford dashboard whereas these parts in the Customline are identical to Mercury.

The Meteor that I had was only the Mainline and was Metallic Fanfare Maroon. I purchased the car in 1954 from another Ham Radio buddy of mine. He was one of the most notable radio personalities here on the west coast at that time, a fellow by the name of Wally Garrett of Radio Station CKNW (New Westminster). Wally had bought the car new from McLennan Motors in New Westminster and decided to upgrade to one of the newer models in 1954.

CHAPTER SIXTY-TWO

1952 Studebaker in Prince Edward Island for $80

The Studebaker Corporation had good reason to celebrate in 1952. The company had been formed one hundred years earlier when Henry and Clem Studebaker of South Bend, Indiana, began building covered wagons to cash in on the westward tide of settlement following the California gold rush of 1849.

Larry Hughes of Moncton, New Brunswick, once owned a 1952 Studebaker:

> I started Grade Twelve at Summerside High School in P.E.I. in the fall of 1965. My dad was in the RCAF stationed at CFB Summerside at that time. I was going to turn eighteen in November and decided it was time for me to have a car. I ended up with a blue 1952 Studebaker Champion with suicide doors, a heater under the front

1952 Studebaker Champion four-door sedan in the sales brochure. The Champion had a flathead 6-cylinder engine and the Commander had an overhead-valve V-8. Ken McGee of Goderich, Ontario, supplied me with a copy of the original 1952 Studebaker sales brochure. Here is what it says: "Studebaker again steps out ahead with advanced new styling for discriminating car buyers. Motoring's newest of the new is the swept-back aerodynamic design that distinguishes the brilliant performing 1952 Studebaker Commander V-8s and the value-packed Studebaker Champions of the low price field... This newest Studebaker tells you instantly that it's your kind of car — styled to step up your spirits — designed to thrill you every mile you drive."

seat, and a three-speed manual transmission with the gearshift on the steering column. Under the hood was a flathead six of 169 cubic inches cranking out 85 horsepower. I paid $80 for the car (which worked out to almost one dollar per horsepower).

I drove it to school on and off for a few months. Because I had a car, I was popular, but for the wrong reason. Smoking was not allowed on school property, but anyone with a car could smoke in their own car. I didn't smoke, but my car soon became a place for my newfound friends to gather legally, so to speak.

My memory tells me that the future Miss Canada of 1968, Carol McKinnon, sat in my car. I do not remember her smoking, but some of her friends did.

Larry's 1965 P.E.I. license plates carried the slogan "Garden of the Gulf," which was changed to "Garden Province" the following year. His car was probably built in Hamilton, Ontario. The Studebaker Corporation opened a branch plant in that city in August 1948 and it remained in production until 1966, a full two years after the American parent company ceased production. Today, several clubs devoted to the preservation of Studebakers are thriving, among them being the Studebaker Drivers Club. Their website is *www.studebakerdriversclub.com*.

The first gasoline-powered car appeared on the island in 1904, but the P.E.I. farming community was fond of horses and buggies and did not welcome these new contraptions. Automobiles were actually banned from the island's roads in 1908 even though there were only nine cars on the island. Four years later, they were permitted but with restrictions. Not until 1919 were automobiles granted the freedom of the island.

CHAPTER SIXTY-THREE

Three Brothers, Three Wives, and a 1953 Chevy

*J*ohn Beare of Kanata, Ontario, shares his story:

My first car was a blue 1953 Chevrolet One-Fifty two-door. I bought it in Winnipeg in the summer of 1957 from my eldest brother for the princely sum of $550. He had purchased it in 1956 for $1400 and courted the girl who became his wife in it. Soon after their marriage he was to be posted to Germany with the Canadian army.

After four years at the Royal Military College in Kingston, I was back home in Winnipeg en route to the University of British Columbia to complete my degree. I drove the Chevy to Vancouver and noticed that the engine smoked quite a bit from the oil breather and used a lot of oil.

In Vancouver, I stayed at a boarding house and one of the other boarders was a diesel mechanic. We, mostly he, took the engine apart in the backyard and found a broken piston ring in one of the cylinders. My friend honed out a scratch in the cylinder, fitted an

All three Beare brothers courted their wives in the same 1953 Chevrolet One-Fifty two-door sedan, but not at the same time! For 1953, Chevrolet came in three series: the modestly priced One-Fifty, the medium-priced Two-Ten, and the top-of-the-line Bel Air. Under the hood was Chevrolet's legendary overhead-valve 6-cylinder engine, first on the market in 1929 to compete with Henry Ford's Model A. Twenty-four years later, Chevrolet was still competing with Ford and still winning.

oversized piston to the defective cylinder, installed new chrome rings for all the cylinders, had the valves ground, and reassembled my 6-cylinder overhead valve engine.

I was a naval officer at the time. Naturally, since I was on the west coast the Navy posted me to Halifax. While driving through New Brunswick, I missed a turn in the dark and ended up with the rear end straddling a ditch and the car at right angles to the road. Another car came along. The driver had a chain, pulled my car out of the ditch, and offered me a beer. That was my introduction to Maritime hospitality.

In Halifax with the '53 Chevy, I met and courted the girl who became my wife. Shortly after we were married, I was posted to England for a year. Before we left for England, I sold the Chevy to my next elder brother, who was in Halifax with the naval reserve. With the Chevy he courted and married the girl who became his wife.

Finally in 1963, with the body rusting out and with sheeting to cover the holes in the floor and with over four hundred thousand miles on the odometer, my brother sold the Chevy to the St. John's-Ravenscourt Cameron Highlanders cadet corps in Winnipeg. It was used for about two years teaching cadets the basics of motor mechanics. Even after being "decommissioned," as they say in the navy, the faithful Chevy performed a useful service.

CHAPTER SIXTY-FOUR

Wayne Chambers Brush-Painted His 1953 Ford

W ayne Chambers reads this column in the *Mississauga News*. His first car was a 1953 Ford two-door with standard transmission and AM radio. He bought it from his mother in 1961 for $500 when he graduated from Huron Park Secondary School in Woodstock, Ontario, and began working as a Bank Junior in Drumbo. His parents had purchased the car in 1958 from Mr. Porter, an Eastwood machine shop owner.

Wayne Chambers (right) and friend Jim Virtue on the fender of his 1953 Ford on a fishing and camping weekend near Goderich, Ontario. Note the wide whitewalls, among the last ones sold retail in 1961 as the new narrow whitewalls became more popular. After two failed attempts at creating a company to manufacture automobiles, Henry Ford finally succeeded in realizing his dream on June 16, 1903, when he oversaw the birth of the Ford Motor Company. At first, Ford did not build all the parts that went into his cars. The Dodge brothers supplied the engines, and they were transported from the Dodge factory to the Ford factory through the streets of Detroit on wagons hauled by teams of horses. In 1953, the Ford Motor Company celebrated its fiftieth anniversary, and a commemorative medallion was mounted in the hub of the steering wheel of every Ford built during that model year.

When brand new, the car was owned by an American tourist visiting Ontario. He was in an accident near Woodstock and, rather than take the car home, sold it to Mr. Porter. The car had a 6-cylinder engine with overdrive. This was a car that few people in Canada knew existed. Ford of Canada only built 8-cylinder engines until 1956. Recalls Wayne:

> The front fender had a dent in it and I tried to straighten it out with a hammer, then painted the fender with a brush. I then hand-painted the other three fenders and the body a light green, leaving the roof, hood, and trunk the original dark Sherwood Green.
>
> Being young and naive about maintenance, I neglected to check the oil, and on a long trip late at night, the oil light came on. I continued home, but had to have the engine rebuilt by Mr. Porter at a cost of $280.92. I then had my odd-coloured car repainted with a white roof and mint green body, which I thought looked really sharp. The body shop owner was not happy at having to remove all my thick, streaky brush painting.
>
> After my first bank transfer to Norwich, I saw some new cars being unloaded at Gare Motors, the local GM dealership. I was admiring a 1963 Pontiac Strato-Chief when car salesman Lynn Bell came along, and before I knew it, I had signed a purchase agreement to buy it for $3079.25 with my '53 Ford as my trade-in for $459.25.
>
> The car dealer sold it to my uncle for the same amount they allowed me. He needed a truck more than a car and it didn't stand up to the farm abuse such as removing the trunk lid to haul feed and bales of hay. The last I heard of it, my uncle had sold it to a young mechanic near Blackwater, who thought he had a real treasure.

CHAPTER SIXTY-FIVE

Dad Gets Caught Drag Racing in Detroit

Malloy ("Mal") Zahara grew up in Windsor, Ontario, and now lives in Leamington. His first car was a 1941 Ford coupe purchased off a used-car lot in Windsor when he was only sixteen. He knew his parents would disapprove so he parked it a block away from

1953 Monarch two-door sedan in the sales brochure. This is what Mal Zahara's Monarch looked like before he customized it.

Malloy Zahara is standing beside his first car, a 1941 Ford business coupe. No pictures were taken of his 1953 Monarch. He was too busy driving it!

their house. Dad soon got wind of it and made Mal return it to the lot where he bought it.

In 1955 Mal began working at the Chrysler plant and bought a nice 1953 Monarch two-door sedan. Not content with having it stock, he frenched the headlights, put an air scoop in the hood, and installed exhaust headers on the flathead V-8, hot ignition, copper head gaskets for higher compression, dual exhausts, Hollywood mufflers, traction bars for better grip on takeoff, whitewall tires with the loudest squeal, spinner wheel discs, big long bubble skirts, and a continental kit with a rear bumper from an Oldsmobile turned upside down. His dad did not share his enthusiasm for all these changes.

Then one day his dad wanted to visit his brother in Detroit, but his own car was down for repairs. He borrowed Mal's car and headed for the border, crossing over into Detroit through the tunnel under the Detroit River. The echo-chamber effect of the tunnel made the Hollywood mufflers sound twice as loud.

After emerging from the tunnel on the Detroit side, he began driving along Jefferson Avenue toward his brother's place. At the first red light, another car pulled up beside him and began revving up its engine. The driver, seeing Mal's car all customized, figured Mal's dad would enjoy a drag race. The light turned green and away went the other car with tires squealing while Mal's dad slowly crossed the intersection.

At the next red light, the other car was there, waiting for him. Same routine. It took off and Mal's dad pulled away from the light like a ninety-year-old. After three or four red lights like this, Mal's dad decided to teach this young punk a lesson. The light turned green, Mal's dad rammed his foot to the floor, the car took off like a rocket, and he was pulled over by the police. The other guy got away.

Mal's dad did not get a ticket but did get a lecture from the Detroit police officer who did not appreciate someone coming over from Canada and racing on Detroit streets. Also, those noisy mufflers were illegal. He got off with a warning, but was Dad ever mad!

CHAPTER SIXTY-SIX

He Customized a Brand New 1953 Plymouth Club Coupe

Bob Pursel was born in 1931 in Leamington, Ontario. His automotive adventures began at age five in a pedal-powered car with the front end resembling a Chrysler Airflow. Even at this early age, Bob was showing a preference for Chrysler-built automobiles.

In his teens, he drove an old 1937 Dodge ("Man, what a car!" he wrote in his photo album). He and two buddies left town in July 1950 for a holiday excursion through Ontario, Quebec, New York, and Vermont, covering 1,600 miles (2,575 kilometres) in the old car. That old Dodge delivered twenty-eight miles per gallon of gas, but used about eight gallons of oil! Bob had to add a quart of oil every fifty miles (thirty-two quarts in all), but the car took them there and brought them home.

By now he was working at the local A&P grocery store in town, where he saved enough money to order his first new car on November 13, 1952. It arrived January 30, 1953 at Hyatt Motors. Bob says, "She was worth waiting for."

The proud new owner of this new 1953 Plymouth Cranbrook club coupe took several photos of the car after putting 1,100 miles on the

Bob Pursel's brand new customized 1953 Plymouth Cranbrook, "the smartest automobile in town."

odometer. Bob then wrote the following information in his family photo album: "Fully-equipped factory equipment includes heater-air-conditioning unit, undercoating, back-up lights, directional signals, and automatic door and glove box lighting. Extra equipment includes inside-controlled spotlight, lighted auto compass, 8-tube Motorola push-button radio, top-of-door side mirrors, and whitewalls."

Even though the car was brand new, Bob proceeded to customize it into "the smartest automobile in town." In his own words, here is what he did:

> A two-tone paint job in gleaming black with light-blue roof, and chrome rear window dividers gives her a hardtop convertible look with the safety and tightness of a coach. The hood is completely shaved and headlights are equipped with chrome "eyelids." At the rear, the trunk lid is completely shaved and equipped with a dash-controlled electric deck latch, chrome licence-plate frame lowered to the bumper, blue dot tail lights, and twelve-inch stainless cans on the tailpipes. Speed equipment includes a Mallory hot ignition and reworked exhaust system.

Under Bob's hood was the factory-installed flathead 6-cylinder with 218 cubic inches cranking out 100 horsepower in stock form. This engine had been used in Plymouths since 1942 and was both economical and reliable.

By purchasing his 1953 Plymouth brand new, Bob Pursel helped the Chrysler Corporation achieve its best year ever with 1.27 million cars built for the 1953 model year (including Dodge, DeSoto, and Chrysler cars, as well as Plymouth).

CHAPTER SIXTY-SEVEN

1954 Cadillac in Ontario Since New

John Brennan of Blenheim, Ontario, is the proud owner of an all-original 1954 Cadillac Series 62 four-door sedan. He purchased this classic beauty in May 2008 and knows the history of the car dating back to the day it was sold new.

The first owner, George Franklin Young, purchased this car from Maclean Motor Sales in Welland, Ontario, on Saturday, May 1, 1954. It came with no radio, just a factory installed delete plate on the dash. Exactly seven years later (May 1, 1961), a new set of tires were installed. The odometer by then showed 45,768 miles.

The car later went into storage for twenty years and was then purchased by Delbert Brough of Wiarton, Ontario, on May 17, 1999. It was now forty-five years old and had gone approximately seventy-four thousand miles.

It was later sold to the current owner, John Brennan, on May 23, 2008, with 82,240 miles. Says John, "It seems all transactions on this car always happened in May."

John Brennan's 1954 Cadillac Series 62 four-door sedan. Note the licence plate: 54CADDY.

Cadillac for 1954 had an all-new body with a "Panoramic" wrap-around windshield and "Dagmars" on the front bumpers (named for a well-endowed movie actress of that era). And with its wide whitewall tires, sparkling chrome, and Cabot Gray finish, this car is a knockout.

The modest tailfins on the rear fenders were a sign of things to come as cars of the late fifties sprouted tailfins that made cars look like spaceships. Tailfins first appeared on Cadillac in 1948 and were reportedly inspired by the Lockheed P-38 "Lightning" pursuit fighter. GM stylist Bill Mitchell said, "From a design standpoint, the fins gave definition to the rear of the car for the first time. They made the back end as interesting as the front and established a long-standing Cadillac styling hallmark."

The tailfin on the driver's side of John's 1954 Cadillac served another function as well, as I discovered years ago while pumping gas after school at an Esso station in Toronto. If you press the round reflector just below the tail light, the entire tail light housing swings up on a hinge to reveal the gas-filler cap.

The gasoline feeds power to the overhead-valve V-8 engine under the hood of John's Cadillac. With 331 cubic inches, it cranks out a very respectable 230 horsepower.

While growing up in Toronto in the 1950s, John remembers his Uncle Joe taking everyone for a ride in his gold-coloured 1955 Cadillac Eldorado convertible (top down, of course). That's when John promised himself that he too would someday own a Cadillac. Now he has one, and it's a beauty!

CHAPTER SIXTY-EIGHT

1954 Chevrolet Hardtop Had No Second Gear

Ken Taylor has fond memories of a car he owned as a teenager in London, Ontario.

In June 1963, I was eighteen and needed a car since I had just sold my 1948 Ford coupe. One evening my cousin Don Taylor and his wife Carol and I drove down to St. Thomas to look at cars.

We stopped at a GM dealer called Disbrowe Motors on the main street, and that's where I fell in love with a beautiful 1954 Chevy Bel Air Sport Coupe. It was a two-door hardtop in light green with a dark green top and dark green rear fender insert panels.

It had the famous "Blue Flame" inline-six cylinder engine of 235.5 cubic inches and 115 horsepower with the three-speed manual transmission on the steering column. I paid $350 cash for that nine-year-old Chevy, a lot of money when you have been making $1 an hour for a fifty-four-hour week!

While attending the Ontario Agricultural College in Guelph in 1963, I drove my friends Doug and Ken Goudy back and forth on

1954 Chevrolet Sport Coupe in the sales brochure.

weekends so that they could help their dad on the farm and I could help my dad with his greenhouse. We all chipped in $2 each for gas, and this kept us going all week.

I always parked my Chevy on a slight hill behind our apartment during the week at the college because on Friday night after school when we were ready to go home to London, I had to make sure we could push the Chevy downhill in case the battery was dead after sitting idle all week.

One very cold winter night in 1964, I couldn't get the Chevy started, so I had my dad pull me down Barker Street with a chain. Just as I took my foot off the clutch to start the engine, I stripped second gear and from that time on, I had to drive my Chevy from first to third gear because I didn't have any money to repair second gear.

I remember getting stuck in a mudhole one night and I couldn't get out. So I asked my new girlfriend at the time (who is now my wife Mary of forty-four years) if she would get behind the wheel while I got out to push.

Well, we got the Chevy out, but my new beige khakis and new desert boots were covered in mud. Great memories!

CHAPTER SIXTY-NINE

Adventures with Granny's Two Morris Minors

*P*hyllis Wagorn reads my "Old Car Detective" column in the EMC Ottawa South *newspaper.*

In 1955, my grandmother, who was born and raised in England, decided at age fifty-seven to learn how to drive a car. She bought a nice new Morris Minor and the lessons began.

It took several months for my dad to teach her how to shift gears and learn the rules of the road. Eventually, he said she was ready to go solo. Her first trip alone was to be a nice drive in the country to have a picnic and do some painting. Heading out of town, she noticed how friendly the other drivers were. Everyone was waving at her and she back at them. After a while she realized she was driving down the wrong side of the road.

Then to her horror she saw a big hill ahead of her. As she approached the top, the car stalled (shifting gears was not as easy as she had hoped). She put on the brake, got out of the car and walked around it, trying to figure out what to do next. Suddenly a truck came by and took the door completely off. She had to walk to a phone and call her driving instructor (my dad!) to come and retrieve the door and drive her home.

Granny's first Morris Minor, a 1955 model.

My grandmother kept that car for several years. She used to drive up to Algonquin Park to paint and would sleep in the car for weeks at a time. At the time, I was only eight and was never allowed to go in the car with her. But my granny and I were very close and one day in 1959 at the cottage, she invited me to go with her to a farmer's field where she would paint.

When we reached the field, she told me it was time I learned how to drive and she would teach me. She told me to drive across the hay field to the far side where she was going to paint. It was difficult to see over the dash and the hay was three feet high but she said if you don't want to stall, you have to drive very fast. All of a sudden we crashed into a pile of stone and were stuck. We had to walk back to get help from my dad. I was grounded for a long time for "driving" with my granny.

She kept the car another few years, then smashed it up (not her fault, of course). When Granny bought her second Morris Minor in 1961, she decided there was too much traffic on the road and gave the car to my parents. Every weekend, as soon as Dad finished work, we would all pile into "ole Bessie" and head for the cottage.

There were five of us kids, my mom and dad, a dog, and enough provisions for the weekend (which always included a case of beer). Because I was so small, I got to sit on the case. We later got a duck that had to go with us to the cottage. And later, my grandmother thought that because it was her car, she should go, too. Wow! How we did it I do not know but to this day I cannot remember being cramped.

We drove "ole Bessie" for many years. My dad was working the late shift and as everyone knows, Ottawa is known for the cold and the snow. He rigged up an electric heater since Bessie was not equipped with one and hung it from the rear view mirror and plugged it into a long extension cord. All he had to do was go out and plug it in about twenty minutes before driving home.

One cold morning in 1962, the year we had a record snowfall, one of his coworkers came in yelling "ole Bessie" was on fire! Dad went out and put the fire out and Bessie was still roadworthy. We decided she needed some sprucing up, so my dad said I could paint her any colour I wanted. Out came all the old cans of paint I could find. We painted big eyes on the front with a big smile and multi-colours all over her. She even had a tail sticking out of the boot. Bessie was a beauty and admired by all.

She was finally put to rest, but we have nothing but good memories of her and all the adventures we had. Those were the "good ole days" and "ole Bessie" was always considered part of the family.

CHAPTER SEVENTY

Born and Died in Hamilton: Allan Avery's 1955 Studebaker

1955 Studebaker Champion sedan in the sales brochure.

Allan Avery and his buddy Bob Kerr (with pipe) on the trunk lid of Allan's 1955 Studebaker Champion.

*A*llan Avery lives today in Dundas, Ontario. Here is his story.

I bought my first car at the end of summer in 1963, a 1953 Ford Mainline sedan V-8 for $75. The tires were bald, the engine smoked, and the rear doors flew open on sharp turns. But none of that concerned me because, as a teenager, all that really mattered was if the radio worked! Then the engine seized up and I scrapped it for $25.

This pleased my dad, who worked at the local Studebaker plant. A few months later, he lined up a job interview for me in the office. The interviewer was a chap named Fred, who asked how I was going to get to work if I got the job. He was selling his 1955 Studebaker Champion. I took the car for a road test and bought it for $125, which I thought would help me land that office job.

It was now the spring of 1964 and after owning the car for a week, Fred called to say the prospective job was put on hold pending the outcome of the plant's shaky future. It was about this time we heard the news of the closing of the plant in South Bend, Indiana. Within two years, the Hamilton plant closed for good, putting over eight hundred employees, including my dad and brother, out of work.

That was grim news for the local economy. But I will never forget those Studebaker "Open Houses" back in the fifties when employees and their families swarmed the plant, gazing at the various production Hawks, Presidents, Champions, and Larks while feasting on hot dogs and ice cream. The Studebaker Corporation put on great Christmas parties for all the employees and their families, too. Those days are gone.

My aqua-coloured 1955 Studey came with a vertical dashboard, an oil bath air cleaner, and a 186-cubic-inch engine, which certainly was not a power plant, but it did get me around, including several summer trips to Leamington to visit my buddy's grandmother. Toward the end of the year, on one of those trips, the engine began to smoke and the mains started screeching. A farmer gave us some used tractor oil, which got us back to Hamilton, where I sold the car to a wrecker for $35.

My next car was a 1959 Dodge with a V-8 engine and push-button tyranny. It was a great car but I will never forget that old '55 Studey that was born and died right here in Canada's Studebaker capital, Hamilton.

CHAPTER SEVENTY-ONE

VW Convertible in Vancouver with Wooden Dipstick

T he late Bob Cartlidge was a lawyer for many years in his home town of Leamington, Ontario. In December 1969, he decided to give the west coast a try and joined a law firm in Vancouver. He found lodgings in the east end of the city, but public transit was unreliable. For the first time in his life, he needed to buy a car.

A neighbour had a very weather-beaten old clunker he was willing to sell for "only $250." And so, in April 1970, Bob became the dubious owner of a Volkswagen convertible that was, as he recalls, "at least fifteen years old." That would date it back to around 1955, making it perhaps the first VW convertible in British Columbia, if not all of Canada.

"It was khaki green with a convertible top that resembled army surplus canvas. The rear window was yellow and cracked and I had to use my rear-view mirror to change lanes. The four-speed transmission had a floor-mounted shift lever but the lever and transmission did not always work as a team. It had no radio and barely had a heater," as Bob recalls with a shiver. "The car had a musty smell whether the top was

Volkswagen convertible in the sales brochure.

up or down, and in heavy rains, I should have opened an umbrella inside the car."

Bob's VW had no gas gauge, but did come with a factory-installed wooden dipstick. The gas went in at the front under the hood (engine in the rear!) but Bob cannot recall ever putting the gas in by himself. This was in the days before self-serve when a cheerful attendant put in your gas, cleaned your windshield, and checked your oil and tires.

During the summer of 1970, Bob moved to the North Shore where driving up and down steep hills put an added strain on the old Volkswagen.

While heading home from work one day, he slowly chugged to the crest of the Lions Gate Bridge. Just after reaching the top, he applied the brakes for the downward descent. No brakes! The pedal went right to the floor with horror-stricken Bob rapidly gaining speed. He yanked up the emergency brake and stopped only inches from the car in front.

He slowly crept off the bridge in first gear and turned into the first car dealership he saw. They sold British sports cars and put Bob behind the wheel of a brand new MGB convertible for "only $3000." Without even a backward glance at his first car, Bob put the MGB in gear and stepped on the gas. It turned out to be not as good as it looked, but that's another story.

CHAPTER SEVENTY-TWO

Another 1956 Ford Convertible Forty-Eight Years Later

Walter Strilec grew up in Toronto and bought his first new car from Thorncrest Motors, a Ford-Monarch dealership on Dundas Avenue West near Islington. It was a 1955 Ford Crown Victoria in "cherry pink and apple blossom white" (which, incidentally, was the title of a hit song that year). A year later, he decided he needed something more exciting and traded in his '55 at that same dealership for a new fire-engine-red 1956 Ford Sunliner convertible.

A year and a half later, he joined the United States Air Force and sold his convertible. In the years that followed, he saw many old cars at shows and swap meets and always found himself on the lookout for another 1956 Ford convertible. Then one day in 2005, while looking at a display of collector cars at the Imperial Palace in Las Vegas, Walter's wife saw a magazine ad offering a 1956 Ford convertible for sale in Arkansas.

It was in good solid condition and partially restored. Walter arranged for a man in North Carolina to complete the restoration and the work was finished by the spring of 2008. In the summer of that year, Walter drove his car to southern Ontario to visit his son and

Walter Strilec with the 1956 Ford convertible he owns today. It has a Thunderbird V-8 engine.

daughter. He brought it one night to the local A&W cruise night here in my hometown of Leamington and that is where I met Walter and saw his car for the first time.

It's gorgeous in coral and white with a new white convertible top and wide whitewall tires. I was thirteen years old in the fall of 1955 when these cars first came out, and I can still see myself looking through a showroom window at one of these dazzling beauties. It was America's most popular convertible for the 1956 model year with 58,147 built compared with 41,268 for Chevrolet and 6,735 for Plymouth.

If you were buying a new Ford in 1956, you had three overhead-valve V-8 engines to choose from, all numbered based on their cubic-inch displacement: 272, 292, and 312. A 6-cylinder engine of 223 cubic inches was also available. The two-seater Thunderbird for 1956 employed the 292 or 312, and if your regular Ford had one of these engines, a Thunderbird insignia appeared on the front fenders ahead of the wheel openings. That way you could tell your neighbours that your car had a "Thunderbird engine."

Ford styling changed dramatically for 1957, making the '55s and '56s unique and instantly recognizable today, over fifty years after they were manufactured.

CHAPTER SEVENTY-THREE

An Engine Transplant He Will Never Forget

*K**eith Mosher of Westport, Ontario, wrote in with his story.*

In the fall of 1965 I purchased a 1957 Chev 210 two-door 6-cylinder standard transmission car in Ottawa. Home was in Shubenacadie, Nova Scotia (a small town between Truro and Halifax), and in the spring of 1966, with the school year over, I drove the car home. Had to be careful it had enough oil but all went well.

During the summer I purchased a 327 V-8 engine for my car and installed it with a new clutch and dual exhausts. All work was done on a dirty gravel floor. When Dad and I went to start it up, the engine ran, but the car would not move. The car was towed to the local garage, where the transmission was removed and the proper throw-out bearing installed. No more transmission problems.

1957 Chevrolet Two-Ten two-door sedan in the sales brochure.

The engine burned way too much oil for having new rings and bearings. The mechanic brother of the person who sold the engine to me took the oil pan off and discovered that the pistons on one bank were installed backwards. Another problem solved. The engine still had valve seal problems and always started with a big cloud of white smoke. I always needed to watch the oil pressure. The engine also would not turn over when hot. This was never solved. Anyway, it was a V-8 and sounded real nice.

Now back to Ottawa and another year in school. This time somewhere in Maine, a clanking sound turned out to be most of a leaf spring falling off. Fifteen dollars and a one-day delay got the leaf spring replaced.

The first weekend in Ottawa the car visited St. Jovite for the first-ever Can-Am race and promptly overheated. A 6-cylinder rad with no fan shroud for the transplanted V-8 caused the problem. Back in Ottawa, one bank of cylinders was cold and the other hot, probably a head gasket causing spark plug fouling.

The body was so bad that the passenger side door post was no longer connected to the rocker panel (the driver's side was fine). The car sat for the winter. I sold the car in the spring for nothing as long as the buyer left the engine and clutch with me (had expectations of doing something with it). Two months later my landlady wanted the engine out of the garage. I sold the engine and clutch to an Ottawa speed shop for $50. My next car was a new black 1967 289 four-speed notchback Mustang, to this day still close to the best of all the cars I have owned.

CHAPTER SEVENTY-FOUR

1958 Nash Metropolitan for Ten Dollars

Terry Webb lives in Brampton, Ontario. He got an amazing deal on a car parked in a field forty-five years ago:

> The first car I ever owned was a cute little '58 Nash Metropolitan purchased in 1966 for the princely sum of $10, which I had saved from my paper-route earnings. The little "scooter car" had beckoned to me from a field behind a repair shop where it had been left derelict. An auto wrecker's battery and a little coaxing brought the four cylinders to life.
>
> Because it had no plates, my friends drove their cars box-style front and rear while I struggled with the three-on-the-tree shifter to get home with the car without the local constabulary spotting me. That's when I discovered, much to my buddy's rear bumper's chagrin, that the brakes needed pumping up on the pedal to function.
>
> Once safely ensconced in my folks' driveway, I proceeded to fix her up. Brakes be damned, what she

The Nash Metropolitan came in two body styles: hardtop and convertible.

needed was wide white Port-a-walls on the wheels and a gallon of white CIL house paint to cover the surface rust and turn the thing into a real babe magnet.

The "back seat" was the size and comfort of a deacon's bench. Making out in it at Marie Curtis Park in Long Branch near Toronto required contortionist expertise and resulted in window-slamming charley horses and perpetual virginity! Still, I loved that little car and found more excitement owning it than any brand new car I have bought in my older boomer years.

My buddy and I had American girlfriends in Buffalo (are there any other kind?) and so we sojourned across the border to visit them. (By the way, Denise, if you're still alive, give me a call!) Anyway, Ron, who was driving, forgot to pump the brakes and we coasted clear past the border guard with his mouth agape. Two hours later and after a complete vehicular inspection and a scrutinizing interrogation, we were allowed to proceed.

Like most young lads' first cars, the little Nash had pros and cons. The good news is that I got thirty-five miles to the gallon. The bad news is it was Loblaws Shur Flo bulk motor oil.

With bodies built in England and fitted with Austin engines, the Nash Metropolitan first went on sale in the fall of 1953. It rode on an eighty-five-inch wheelbase and weighed about eighteen hundred pounds. In April 1956, the Metropolitan 1500 was launched with a more powerful engine that pushed the top speed up to almost eighty miles per hour.

Styling was updated along with garish two-tone paint schemes that one stylist likened to Neapolitan ice cream. Production ended in 1962, partly due to competition from the compact cars introduced by the Big Three in 1960.

CHAPTER SEVENTY-FIVE

The Second Time Around: Bob Crocker's 1958 Pontiac Parisienne

Born in 1938, Bob Crocker grew up in the east end of Toronto. In 1954 he got his driver's licence and since then has owned sixty vehicles. Two of his favourites are in this story.

In 1960 he spotted an ad for a 1958 Pontiac Parisienne two-door hardtop. "I went to look at the car," recalls Bob, "and it was love at first sight. It was only two years old and just like new. The original finish was Burma Green and Calypso Green.

> Under the hood was the big block 348-cubic-inch V-8, which was new that year. It was a Chev V-8 because all Canadian-built Pontiacs back then had Chev engines. The car had dual exhausts and a four-barrel carb. Lots of horsepower, but it used a lot of gas. The only item I added was a pair of Foxcraft fender skirts.

Bob Crocker owns this 1958 Pontiac Parisienne two-door hardtop today. It is almost identical to the one in which he courted his wife Carol fifty years ago. The only noticeable difference is the reversal of colour with the Burma Green and Calypso Green.

Sometime after that, I met my future wife at a YMCA dance. I think I made quite an impression on Carol when I drove her home in the Parisienne. She soon became my fiancée and we decided to wait a full year before getting married so we could save money for a small house.

Unfortunately, this meant selling my '58 Pontiac. I sold it in 1962 to a fellow who was moving out west but I didn't keep his name. I wonder if the car is still around.

If it is, there might still be some telltale signs identifying it as the 1958 Pontiac Bob sold over forty years ago: "I had the air cleaner and valve covers chrome-plated, along with the oil filler cap and other small engine items. The car had a Wonderbar radio with a rear seat speaker, power windows, power steering, and power brakes. It also had a large exterior mirror on the driver's door, and both doors had stainless-steel edging to protect from paint chips. The mileage on the car when I sold it was around fifty thousand miles."

Bob Crocker is now retired and living in Tillsonburg, Ontario. The story of his 1958 Pontiac first appeared in my "Old Car Detective" column in *Old Autos* newspaper. Two days after the story appeared, a man in Yorkton, Saskatchewan, phoned Bob to say a 1958 Pontiac matching the description of his car was T-boned in an accident in Yorkton about twenty years ago. Further investigation failed to determined if that was Bob's car.

Several other leads came in from across Canada, and even one from the United States, but nothing turned up. Then Bob found a 1958 Pontiac Parisienne in Quebec almost identical to the one he had owned and in nearly perfect condition. He bought it and is now driving it.

CHAPTER SEVENTY-SIX

Their 1959 Austin-Healey Sprite Actually Had a Floor!

Austin-Healey Sprites with distinctive protruding headlights were built in England from 1958 to 1961. In North America, they were nicknamed "Bug-Eye" and in England "Frog-Eye." A total of 48,999 were built. Here is the story of two of them from Rod Smith, who reads this column in the Ottawa EMC.

In 1970, my parents and their four youngest children moved overseas, leaving my elder brother and me in a rented apartment on Garden Road in Aylmer, Quebec. George was nineteen and enjoying his first year of a teaching career and I was eighteen and struggling to make it out of high school.

Our father, who was with the Department of External Affairs, kindly agreed not to leave us home alone without wheels, so together we searched for something cheap and serviceable. When we stumbled upon a white 1959 Bug-Eye Sprite, common sense flew out the window

Austin-Healey Sprite in the sales brochure.

and all three of us were hooked. After some furious haggling, Father purchased this open-top gem for the grand price of $140.

It was in pretty good shape for a vehicle over ten years old, so George and I polished it up to near showroom condition. Wearing the requisite leather driving gloves, with green Ivy caps snug on our heads and striped scarves whipping in the wind, we drove around our nation's capital, waving gloriously to the drivers of other British sports cars.

A few months later, our "baby" started groaning like a wounded animal and a local mechanic informed us that the engine was shot. Worse than that, he told us that replacement parts were unavailable and that unless we found another Sprite with a serviceable engine to transplant into ours, our glory days were over.

Relatively penniless, we finally found a chap in Touraine, Quebec, who had another '59 Sprite in working order. We haggled and haggled, but this young chap was firm and would not sell his car at any price (could you blame him?).

However, he said he would be happy to look at ours and possibly buy it for spare parts. When he opened the door of our car and exclaimed with glee, "It has a floor!" — George and I knew we had a buyer. His Sprite was rusty and had pieces of plywood riveted in place to keep the seats from falling through to the pavement.

George and I said goodbye to our Sprite for $75 and put that money toward a battleship grey 1960 Chevrolet Biscayne two-door hardtop — but that's another story!

CHAPTER SEVENTY-SEVEN

1959 Corvette in British Columbia: One Owner Since 1972

On June 15, 1972, Gord Bergen of Abbotsford, British Columbia, bought the second car he has ever owned: a faded silver 1959 Corvette with a tired 327 under the hood and 113,000 miles on the odometer. He paid $2000 for it (about five months' wages at the time) and had to sell his first car — a 1970 Cuda 383.

Gord saw it parked in a carport under a tarp. It had not run in nine months. He got it running and it was his only car for the next six months until he bought a winter "beater" to save wear and tear on his newfound pride and joy. In the spring of 1975, after completing some body work and paint, Gord invited Karen for a little cruise in his Vette. A relationship blossomed and they were married in October 1976.

For their honeymoon, they drove the Vette along the Washington–Oregon–California coast down to San Francisco. While driving across the Oakland Bay Bridge, a black limo cruised up beside them, the tinted

Gord and Karen Bergen are all smiles in their 1959 Corvette.

passenger window rolled part way down, a hand with a "thumbs-up" came out and then disappeared and the window closed. The newlyweds never did see the passenger, but enjoyed that memorable moment for young honeymooners just having fun.

In 1977, Gord and Karen drove the Vette to Manitoba for Gord's parents' twenty-fifth anniversary. In 1992, Gord drove his mother-in-law to the church for her second wedding. The Vette has also been present for their daughters' high school graduations and weddings. In 2007, the car went to Manitoba for a cousin's wedding. He met his bride in British Columbia and their first date was in the Vette, so it seemed appropriate to have the car at the wedding.

Friends relate the story of seeing Gord and Karen for the first time in the Corvette with a cute little blond girl riding between them, then realized there was another baby riding along when they pulled the GM Cuddle Seat out from under the dash. Two little girls tucked in for Sunday cruising! Later, as other girls were born, they slipped four of them in for jaunts out for ice cream, but they later outgrew their spots. Now their little grandson is excited to ride in "Papa's Varoom."

In 2010, Gord treated the car to fresh red urethane paint, hood scoop, and flares with black leather interior featuring custom door panels designed by Gord. He also fabricated many engine parts including hand-hammered aluminum fan shroud and handmade air cleaner. With a few exceptions, all the many modifications were done by Gord in his home shop.

Also in 2010, Gord and Karen enjoyed a second honeymoon by driving their Corvette once again down the Washington, Oregon, and California coastline. Gord writes, "The Corvette handled it all with grace and style not unlike the Porsches and new Corvettes we met along the way. Our trip took us as far south as Los Angeles and we visited Disneyland on the hottest day on record. We arrived home safely after 3500 miles of wonderful memories, knowing that we may never drive the Corvette that far from home again. Here we are, all these years later, still enjoying the car. It turns heads and brings big smiles wherever we go. The Corvette has become so woven into the fabric of our family's history, it would be difficult to part with it now."

CHAPTER SEVENTY-EIGHT

His 1960 Meteor Montcalm "Just Short of the Queen Mary"

W*aynne Charlton now lives in Centralia, Ontario. But he hasn't always lived there …*

In 1961, I was living in Aylmer, Ontario, and driving a '61 Vauxhall Victor, not because I wanted to but I had worn out my new '60 Victor driving to work at Supertest in London and chasing an electrician's daughter thirty miles in the opposite direction.

For weeks I had driven by the Aylmer B/A garage and I fell in love with a '60 Meteor Montcalm two-door hardtop with automatic, whitewalls, and radio. The owner of the place sold a few used cars from beside the garage. I stopped in to see her many times. She was black with a red interior, about three times the length of my Vauxhall, and a gross tonnage just short of the Queen Mary. She had seventeen thousand miles on the speedo and a 332 V-8.

Finally, one day I went to my banker and said I wanted to trade up. He said, "How is going from a '61 to a '60 trading up?"

1960 Meteor Montcalm two-door hardtop in the sales brochure and identical to the car purchased by Waynne Charlton in Aylmer, Ontario, in 1961.

I said, "If you melt down that Meteor, you could make three Vauxhalls." I got the loan. She was mine in minutes. I still remember driving it off the lot. That V-8 purred smoother than the family cat on a warm blanket. It was a warm summer day and I rolled all four windows down and drove right up the main street of Aylmer like I had just purchased the Carnation Milk factory, which incidentally closed about that time.

Half a mile from the garage, I met my brother, who was on the road selling for National Grocers at the time. I flashed my lights and we pulled over on opposite sides of the street. With my chest stuck out, almost brushing the steering wheel, he hollered across, "What are you doing driving so-and-so's car?" It turned out my brother knew the previous owner, who had bought the car new and drove it about twenty hours every day since. A chick magnet, it had accumulated way past one hundred thousand miles.

I went right back to the B/A garage. The man who sold it to me said something about "*caveat emptor.*" I didn't know much Latin in those days but I was learning pretty quickly. I drove the Meteor for about a year. Too soon the 332's rings were bypassing some of the Supertest oil. The tailpipe had gone from gray to black and it was time to move up again.

The Meteor was the Canadian version of the Ford and the Montcalm was the top-of-the-line series for 1960.

CHAPTER SEVENTY-NINE

New Hood Ornament on Morris Minor "Woodie"

Danny Bateman was born in 1944 and lives in Leamington, Ontario. He and his wife Jan operated Bateman Stationery on Erie Street South for many years and now run "Make Your Move," a business assisting people in relocating, especially seniors who are downsizing.

In 1965, when Danny started working at his first full-time job, he decided to buy his first car. He found what he was looking for on the used car lot of Wigle Motors: a Morris Minor wood-bodied station wagon. Danny can't remember the year of this exotic vehicle (we're guessing 1961), but he can still remember the "exorbitant" price of $250.

It was a handyman's special. To spruce it up (no pun intended), he painted the wood frame on the sides and back a bright red, as well as the wheel rims. The name "Brutus" just seemed to fit and was painted on both sides. Danny and six of his friends wore red sweat shirts with "Brutus" printed on the front.

Danny Bateman's Morris Minor with his friend Neil Fotheringham on the hood.

Mechanically, Brutus had great strengths and great weaknesses. On Danny's frequent trips from Leamington to Hamilton to visit his future bride, Brutus would get around fifty miles to the gallon. However, in trying to pass transport trucks on Hwy. 401, and even with his foot to the floor, Danny could only get as far as alongside the truck driver's window before the wind resistance stalled his ability to pass and he would have to drop back behind the truck. How humiliating!

Also, there were times Brutus refused to start. That's when Danny had to go to the front, undo one of the two bolts holding up the front licence plate, and let it hang down while he crank-started the engine. Unfortunately, this procedure was necessary one time when Danny was taking his future wife, Jan, out to eat at a restaurant on Main Street in Hamilton. How embarrassing!

Brutus was sold after about a year to a young fellow who neglected to transfer the ownership. Danny was advised of this by the police after the new owner totalled Brutus against a tree (ashes to ashes, wood to wood) in London, Ontario. The end of a legend. Et tree, Brute!

The first Morris arrived on the automotive scene in 1913 and was named for the man who designed and built it: William Morris. After the Second World War, he decided to create a small four-passenger car. It was put into production in 1948.

At first, it was going to be called the Morris Mosquito but was then renamed Morris Minor. Danny Bateman thinks the original name more appropriate because, when he drove around in the summer, mosquitoes often flew in through open windows.

CHAPTER EIGHTY

1962 Plymouth Fury Convertible From Alberta to Nova Scotia

Roger St. Denis and his wife Linda were living near Windsor, Nova Scotia, in 2003 when they spotted an ad in the *Auto Trader* for a 1962 Plymouth Fury convertible in showroom condition. They phoned the seller in Lethbridge, Alberta, and flew out there to look at the car. He met them at the airport in Calgary and drove them to his home, where they saw that the car was exactly as advertised. They bought it and drove it home to Nova Scotia.

Linda had always wanted a convertible and Roger had owned a 1962 Plymouth two-door back in 1970, which he drove at racetracks near his home town of Tilbury, Ontario. That car met a very bizarre end. Roger stored it in the barn on his parents' farm in the fall of 1970, planning to put it back on the road the following spring. Later that fall, the farmer on the next farm used dynamite to get rid of a tree stump on his property.

KABOOM! The stump flew so high into the air it went out of sight, then crashed through the roof of Roger's parents' barn, flattening his

Roger St. Denis with his award-winning 1962 Plymouth Fury convertible at the Leamington Marina.

1962 Plymouth. Thus ended his racing days and he married Linda the following year.

Now fast forward to 2010. Their 1962 Plymouth Fury convertible car is still like new in every detail, including the original push-button automatic transmission. It was reportedly sold new in California and later came to Alberta where it was stored for many years and then restored. When Roger and Linda bought it, a 318 V-8 was under the hood. Roger replaced that engine with a 413 from a motor home and arranged with Armstrong Automotive to bore it out .030 to make it a 426. Now he has enough horsepower to rip the asphalt right off the road.

Roger drove the car to the Graves Island, Nova Scotia, car show on June 25, 2005, where he was astounded to learn he had won two first prizes: Best in Show for Cars 1960–1965, and Best in Show as a Chrysler product. And because he was born on June 25, 1945, he won these trophies on the day he turned sixty!

In 2008, Roger and Linda moved back to Leamington, Ontario, where Roger had worked for the H.J. Heinz Company for thirty-five years. He brings his car frequently to the cruise nights at the local A&W and plans to drive to a big car show in Ohio in 2012, when his car will be fifty years old.

CHAPTER EIGHTY-ONE

1963 Falcon Futura Convertible: First New Car I Wanted to Buy

I t was the spring of 1963, long before I became known as the "Old Car Detective." My twenty-first birthday was rapidly approaching. It would arrive on May 4. A year earlier, I had sold my mechanically challenged 1940 Mercury convertible after the clutch pedal broke off in the middle of a downshift and fell through where the floor used to be and landed on the road.

"Wouldn't it be nice to have a red convertible with nothing wrong with it?" I said to myself as I tried to study for my final exams in my second year as a history student at York University in Toronto. The exams finished a few days before my birthday and I actually passed! Now I could think about more important things. Cars, for example.

When I got my driver's licence in 1958 at age sixteen, I had no desire to own a new car (couldn't afford one, anyway). The new cars back then were big and no young kid owned one. If you drove around town in one, it was your dad's car. Not cool.

Joan Quick's 1963 Falcon Futura convertible parked on the main street of Leamington, Ontario, during the Tomato Fest car show in August 2010.

I desperately wanted to be cool and so I bought the toughest-looking old car I could find. I made it look even tougher by sanding down the shiny red finish and repainting it in charcoal grey primer. All four hub-caps came off and a rope wrapped around the front bumper held the hood down. Whenever I accelerated, the glove compartment door flew open. No one's dad would be caught dead in a car like that, and so, when I finally got it running and on the road, everyone who saw me drive by would automatically know it was *my* car.

But by the spring of 1963, a new car came on the market that I briefly fancied myself driving. It was a Ford Falcon, but not one of those econo-boxes on four wheels when they first came out in 1960. Starting in mid-1963, you could buy a new Falcon Futura Sprint convertible with a 260 cid V-8 cranking out 164 horsepower. Sprints had special trim, bucket seats, a console, and full instrumentation including a 6000 rpm tachometer.

The one I planned to order would have the optional four-speed floor-shift transmission. The American price when new was $2600. Slightly higher in Canada plus 3 percent provincial sales tax.

I had been working every summer since I was fifteen and you would think by twenty-one, I could buy a new car, even though I was still in school. However, the old car I owned for three years had taken a vacuum cleaner to my bank account.

For my twenty-first birthday, I bought a second-hand ten-speed bicycle from a school chum of mine for $60, pedalled my way to school, and soon forgot about the Falcon Futura convertible. I still have the bike. It now sits in the garage on two flat tires.

CHAPTER EIGHTY-TWO

How Cars and Marriage Go Together

C athy McGinnis lived in Barrie, Ontario, until 1957 when she moved with her parents to the west end of Toronto. She attended George R. Gauld Public School and Mimico High School. After graduating in 1962, she worked as a secretary for the Steel Company of Canada.

A wedding was planned for October 9, 1965, but her fiancé had a change of heart and the wedding was cancelled. Cathy used the money from the cancelled wedding to buy her first car: a gleaming black 1964 Chevelle Malibu SS two-door hardtop. She then met a gentleman and was married on October 22, 1966. Since he owned a 1965 Chevrolet Impala, Cathy sold her 1964 Malibu.

They were a one-car family until the early 1970s, when Cathy bought a yellow 1964 Ford Galaxie 500XL convertible with cream interior, black roof, bucket seats, floor-mounted automatic, and a

Cathy McGinnis's first car was her one-year-old 1964 Chevelle Malibu SS two-door hardtop parked in front of her parents' home in Long Branch in the west end of Toronto.

Thunderbird V-8 engine. Cathy loved driving this car. She and the car seemed to suit each other.

For extra ventilation, you could tab down the glass rear window to create an opening between the window and the roof. Her husband tried lowering the top with the rear window partially open. The glass window shattered into thousands of fragments and a costly new rear window had to be installed.

During the winter of 1974, Cathy was driving south on Hwy. 400 from Barrie to Toronto behind a truck in the centre lane. The truck suddenly changed lanes to avoid a slow-moving VW hauling a trailer. Cathy swerved to avoid the VW, clipped the tail light of the trailer, and hit the brakes to slow down. The highway was slushy between lanes and her car began fishtailing. To avoid hitting other cars, she forced her car into the guardrails. When the car stopped, it was facing north in the southbound lane.

Cathy was slightly shaken, but not hurt. As she was being assisted from her car, she heard someone say, "There's someone else in the car!"

Many years later, Cathy is smiling from behind the wheel of a 1964 Malibu at a recent car show in Bothwell, Ontario, sponsored by Old Autos *newspaper.*

They had spotted a wig on the floor of the front seat and thought it was a small child. It was actually Cathy's ash-blonde wig that had fallen off the front seat when the car spun around.

When Cathy telephoned her husband, it seemed he was more concerned about the car and his hockey equipment in the trunk. The marriage had been experiencing some concerns and shortly thereafter they separated with Cathy saying goodbye to the convertible.

In Moncton, New Brunswick, on October 29, 1976, Cathy remarried and her husband was employed by Chrysler Canada. He was entitled to a company car and a leased car. Cathy now drove a new Chrysler vehicle every year.

So in reflection, Cathy bought a GM product (the Malibu) because of a cancelled wedding, sold it to get married to someone else, gave up a Ford product (the Galaxie 500XL convertible) to dissolve that marriage, and then married a man who worked for Chrysler. She had by now driven cars from all the "Big Three" and, it seems that in her life, cars and marriage go together, especially in October.

CHAPTER EIGHTY-THREE

A Baby Boomer Buys a Mustang

D eborah Godin has a charming story to tell about a very special car:

This isn't a story about my first car, or any car from my youth for that matter, but I think it's a good one, nonetheless. The story of how I came to own this car began one day in 2004 when I was talking with a neighbour, and learned quite by accident that he was buying a vintage Mustang.

I was immediately envious, but then he mentioned he wasn't keeping it for himself. He was just going to buy it and flip it. We started talking about it, and to make a long story short, he ended up flipping it to me! I knew the minute he told me the details about it that day that this car was meant for me. Here is how it happened …

Deborah Godin's 1965 Mustang hardtop from the front. The first Mustang rolled off the assembly line in April 1964. It was supposed to go to the Henry Ford Museum in Dearborn, Michigan, but by mistake was shipped to a Ford dealer in St. John's, Newfoundland, who promptly sold it to an airline pilot. The Ford Motor Company tried to buy it back, but the new owner said no because he was having too much fun driving it around the island. Two years later, he agreed to let it go in exchange for a new 1967 Mustang. Now the first Mustang is on display in the Henry Ford Museum after its unexpected two-year sojourn in Newfoundland.

My pony rolled off the assembly line in Dearborn, Michigan, in 1965 — the same year I graduated from high school in Detroit. Maybe even on the same day, who knows? That Mustang was designated to Ford of Canada, so it immediately crossed the border and began its journey westward.

A few years later, I too crossed the border and began moving west. Eventually, the Mustang ended up in a charming little place called Salt Spring Island in British Columbia, and I ended up in High Country, in the Alberta foothills near Calgary.

Down the road from me was the neighbour who was into Mustangs, and who also spent time on Salt Spring Island. One day, he saw the car for sale there, checked it out, found it was in great shape, and set the wheels in motion, literally and figuratively, to bring it to Alberta.

So that is why I believe we were destined to be together, my little pony and me. We both made our journeys over many miles and many years, far from our

Deborah Godin's license plate, DOWADIDY, *was inspired by the Brit band Manfred Mann's big hit in the 1960s: "Do Wah Diddy Diddy".*

common point of origin, finally to be reunited at long last. Recently, I moved from Alberta to Leamington, Ontario, not far from the Windsor/Detroit border. So maybe one day I'll take my pony for a drive back to Dearborn, where it all began.

It's very fitting that Deborah Godin drives a vintage vehicle from the mid-sixties. Her car was born in the middle of the rock 'n' roll explosion, with the Motown sound riding high on the charts. She loved all the music of the day, and has recently written a fascinating book that re-visits all those great songs of yesteryear. It's called *Papa Do Run: A Baby Boomer Looks (and Laughs) at Vintage Rock 'n' Roll*. You can find out more about this great book at *www.deborahgodin.com*.

CHAPTER EIGHTY-FOUR

CALLING ALL OLD CAR STORIES FROM ALL ACROSS CANADA!

Y ou are invited to send in your old car stories and photos for the next book in this series of *Old Car Detective: Favourite Stories*.

The next volume in this series will cover the years from 1925 to 1970. You can email your stories to *billtsherk@sympatico.ca* or write to Bill Sherk, P.O. Box 255, 25 John Street, Leamington, ON, N8H 3W2.

Antique and Classic Car Club of Canada
(*www.acccc.ca*).

Canadian Automotive Historians Association (CAHA)
   Doug Wells
   50 Wimbledon Road
   Guelph, Ontario
   N1H 7N1

Early Ford V-8 Club of America, Southern Ontario RG#149
   Box 21104
   314 Harwood Ave. South
   Ajax, ON L1S 7H2
To subscribe to the club's newsletter, contact *light139@rogers.com*.

Historical Automobile Society of Canada (HASC)
(*www.historical-automobile-society.ca*).

McLaughlin-Buick Club of Canada
   Membership Chairperson
   Robert Ward
   25 York Strett
   RR #1
   Sutton West, Ontario, Canada
   L0E 1R0

Model A Owners of Canada Inc. (Ford)
(*www.modelaowners.com*).

Also by Bill Sherk

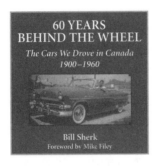

60 Years Behind the Wheel

The Cars We Drove in Canada, 1900–1960

978-1550024654

$24.99

From rumble seats and running boards to power tops and tailfins, *60 Years Behind the Wheel* captures the thrill of motoring in Canada from the dawn of the twentieth century to 1960. There are intriguing stories of cars with no steering wheels, and fascinating photographs of historic vehicles from across the country. From the Studebaker to the Lincoln-Zephyr, from the showroom to the scrapyard, here are over 150 vehicles owned and driven by Canadians.

500 Years of New Words

The Fascinating Story of How, Why, and When Hundreds of Your Favourite Words First Entered the English Language

978-1550025255

$24.99

500 Years of New Words takes you on an exciting journey through the English language from the days before Shakespeare to the first decade of the twenty-first century. All the main entries are arranged not alphabetically, but in chronological order, based on the earliest known year that each word was printed or written down. This book can be opened at any page and the reader will discover a dazzling array of linguistic delights.

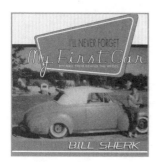

I'll Never Forget My First Car
Stories from Behind the Wheel
978-1550025507
$24.99

In this hilarious collection of stories, *Old Autos* columnist Bill Sherk describes in vivid detail the trials and tribulations of those brave souls who, throwing caution to the wind and money down the drain, made the fateful decision that would forever change the course of their lives. They went out and bought their very first cars. And whether it came from the showroom or the scrapyard, your first car was your ticket of admission into the adult world. Gas, oil, repairs, tow trucks, speeding tickets, insurance, and fender benders would take a vacuum cleaner to your bank account, but you didn't care. You were behind the wheel and on the road.

DUNDURN
www.dundurn.com

What did you think of this book?
Visit www.dundurn.com
for reviews, videos, updates, and more!